Twin of Blackness

Twin of Blackness

a memoir

Clifford Thompson

PITTSBURGH

Autumn House Press Staff
Michael Simms: Founder, Editor-in-Chief, and President
Eva Simms: Co-Founder
Giuliana Certo: Managing Editor
Christine Stroud: Associate Editor
Alison Taverna: Assistant Editor
Ashleigh Fox: Intern
Sharon Dilworth, John Fried: Fiction Editors
J.J. Bosley, CPA: Treasurer
Anne Burnham: Fundraising Consultant
Michael Wurster: Community Outreach Consultant
Jan Beatty: Media Consultant
Heather Cazad: Contest Consultant
Michael Milberger: Tech Crew Chief

 Autumn House Press receives state arts funding support through
a grant from the Pennsylvania Council on the Arts, a state agency
funded by the Commonwealth of Pennsylvania and the National
Endowment for the Arts, a federal agency.

ISBN: 978-1-938769-10-8
Library of Congress: 2015933200

For the old Division Avenue/Ames Street gang, here and gone

Chapters

Prelude   1

1. The Basement of 232, or, Wayne Left Me Undone   3

   Interlude   45

2. Sugar, Muhammad, and Me   47

   Interlude   55

3. Comics, Music, Movies, Novels, and the Limits of Alienation   57

   Interlude   75

4. College and Self-preservation   77

   Interlude   87

5. The Apple and Mrs. O.   93

   Interlude   101

6. Writing, Race, and James Baldwin   103

   Interlude   117

7. The Spanish Tinge   119

   Interlude   133

8. Work   135

   Interlude   139

9. Jazz, Fatherhood, and Albert Murray   141

   Interlude   149

10. Workings of the Heart   151

    Interlude   159

11. Plugdinism   161

Prelude

I have come to think of blackness as my twin. The proof is that we came along at the same time: 1963, the year of my birth, also brought the March on Washington and Martin Luther King Jr.'s "I Have a Dream" speech. I feel toward blackness the way one might toward a twin. I love it, and in a pinch I defend it; I resent the baggage that comes with it; I have been made to feel afraid of not measuring up to it; I am identified with it whether I want to be or not—and never more than when I assert an identity independent of it.

The Basement of 232, or, Wayne Left Me Undone

My Uncle Brock was missing his front teeth and quite a few others besides. I don't know if his drinking caused that—he seemed to drink more than he ate—but it couldn't have helped, just as it didn't add any pounds to his very lean frame. Because he was so lean, he seemed long to me: long limbs, long, medium-brown fingers that often held cigarettes, long, skinny feet in brown loafers and white socks, a long, narrow face. It was a kind face, with a salt-and-pepper mustache and squinty eyes.

The eyes looked down on me one night when I was about ten, as he sat on the side of my small bed. Other relatives who lived nearby were downstairs with my parents, playing cards, drinking, smoking, and laughing. Uncle Brock had heard I was sick and had come to my little room to keep me company, smiling as he talked about girls and this and that in his gentle, whiskey-roughened voice.

Seventeen years or so later, the memory of that voice brought tears to my eyes; it was 1990, I was two hundred miles from that little room and soon to be much farther, and I had just been told about his death.

Usually when I heard Uncle Brock's voice it alternated with the smoother tones of his buddy and brother-in-law, my father. At our dining-room table they would talk about people they knew, or TV shows, or the most recent NASA mission, or movies they wanted to see but—as far as I could tell—never got around to, or the horses. It was Uncle Brock who later went to Laurel racetrack, the scene of my father's death the day before, with the ticket that had been found in my father's wallet. Not untypically, it brought no money.

There is a pairing of voices that reminds me of my father and Uncle Brock's: the sounds of Coleman Hawkins, the original jazz tenor saxophonist, and Roy Eldridge, a luminary of the trumpet. The obvious relish with which they played together, their humor and pizzazz and down-homeness as they traded fours, makes me think of those long-ago conversations between my father and uncle. In my mind, Hawkins—who loomed somewhat larger on the sax than Eldridge did on trumpet—is my father, who had the larger place in my life. Hawkins's mighty tone and pronounced vibrato could make the air seem to tremble, an effect my father's voice could sometimes have, more than he knew, on my insides.

In my mind, it is a short step from thinking of Hawkins and Eldridge to thinking of my father and uncle. In my life, I made the journey the long way around, arriving just in time to save my sanity.

I imagine a film about the Washington, DC, streets where I grew up in the 1960s and '70s. It opens with still, black-and-white shots of hilly Division Avenue, Northeast, in the valley where it intersects with Nannie Helen Burroughs Avenue. As Coleman Hawkins blows a wistful ballad on the soundtrack, maybe "Time on My Hands," we see in turn the wide, wide front window and triangular roof of the Safeway food store (whose building, the last time I passed it, housed a church); next to it, on the corner, the Spic and Span, still closed and bearing the black burn marks from the '68 riots; catty-cornered from there, the Amoco filling station, whose second "o" has fallen off to leave a misspelling of "amok"; near that, the drug store where I bought some of my beloved comic books, in the days when they cost twenty and twenty-five cents; a couple of doors up the block, the Chanese restaurant, part of whose upper-case "A" was removed to leave a slanting "I" when the owners realized their mistake; one or two doors up from there, a bar/lounge that was open all day, giving a view of an interior as black as outer space; close by, Woodson High School and also Ruff's Barber Shop, of the hit-or-miss haircuts; and, on the corners, dotting the sidewalks, standing and talking any time of day, clusters of black men—the unemployed, the unemployable, the semi-employed, the illegally employed.

Now we have a tracking shot, up Division Avenue, past semi-detached brick houses, so many and so similar that we are all but hypnotized when the camera stops to focus on three. The owners of these houses had come decades earlier from rural Virginia and made their way to this block—my mother and father to 232, my Aunt Emma and Uncle Nay to 234, my Aunt Lucy and Uncle Manson to 236; Aunt Catherine and her husband, William Brockenborough (aka Uncle Brock), lived farther up the street and around the corner, in a little pale-green stucco house on Ames Street.

Two-thirty-two and 234 were attached, their interiors mirror images of each other. Between 234 and 236 were twin concrete staircases leading to the backyards. There were no fences separating the backyards of the three houses, and their boundaries were blurry. Our backyard had grass and a couple of trees. Uncle Nay's had wooden horses and other equipment for whatever he was working on or rebuilding—his car, his back porch. But it was Uncle Manson's backyard that contained the creation that defied category, the possible prototype for my own sensibility. Its centerpiece was the shell of an early-1960s tail-fin car, which Uncle Manson had painted pink and half-sunk into the ground. Over it he had constructed a cinderblock arch, and adorning the arch and car were dozens of trinkets and doodads that collectively resembled a swarm of bees frozen in mid-buzz. Here was Americana, folk art, the Roman arch, dime-store merchandise, and workmanship learned in segregated communities of country and city—a crazy brew of race, commerce, classicism, and where-the-hell-did-*that*-come-from, a linked-up hodgepodge of the kind that gets me jazzed up and may be the salvation of us all.

Manson Ligon, born in 1899, was my great-uncle; his brother Robert, who died before I was born, was my mother's father. Robert's widow, Maggie, Manson's sister-in-law and my grandmother, lived with us at 232.

Manson was fairly light-skinned and bald on top with a mustache above pouting lips. That feminine touch was at odds with the rest of him: in my earliest memories he is nearly seventy years old but powerful-looking, with meaty forearms and work-roughened hands, one of which would squeeze yours with great force while the other landed with greater force on your back. ("Well, *hel*-lo, Cliff"—*kapow*.) Any joke would get a laugh out of him—not a chuckle but a crow, one that could reduce small children to tears. His nickname was "Blowgum," because he could talk up a storm, as in, "He sure can blow his gums." I think now that he must have been a bull of a young man in the country, in the days when, as he once told me, he would work until dark and then make his way home through the pitch-black woods with his pistol for protection against whatever or whoever was lurking there. (When night fell in the country in the first decades of the twentieth century, it meant business.) In the city he worked in various industrial kitchens, but by the time I knew him he was retired, with what my mother often called "nothing to do and a lot of time to do it in." (Hence the backyard art.) Then there were his animals. Uncle Manson kept two hunting beagles, mostly—those poor dogs—in a homemade wooden pen; once in a while, let out of the pen, they would crisscross the three backyards in howling brown-and-white blurs. Once, in the backyard, I saw Uncle Manson behead a chicken. I can still hear the chop, still see that bird running around like a . . .

I remember Manson's wife, my Aunt Lucy, as a good-hearted, very talkative woman who wore pant suits, dark, curly wigs, and bright red nail polish chipped almost to the point of vanishing. Manson and Lucy had no kids but seemed to take care of everybody else's; they raised a couple as their own, and a lot of girls, some of them my classmates, hung around their house or on their front porch after school. Apparently other kinds of people had once hung out there, too: one day in the late 1970s or early 1980s I opened the door at 232 to a well-dressed older man who was looking for "Lucy Ligon, the one who used to mess with the numbers."

One of Uncle Manson's brothers, Otis, was the father of Uncle Nay; Nay was married to Emma, one of my father's older sisters—making Nay my uncle on one side of the family and my first cousin once removed on the other. (Aunt Catherine, Uncle Brock's wife, was my father's older sister too.) Uncle Nay was a lot darker-skinned than Uncle Manson; he was smaller and quieter, too, but no less manly. (If you've ever read or seen Larry McMurtry's *Lonesome Dove*, Uncle Nay was Woodrow Call to Uncle Manson's Gus McCrae.) One of Uncle Nay's nicknames was "Pepper," I think because he came from Culpepper, Virginia. Whenever I think of him, the word "work" comes to mind. A retired cement mason—he had helped erect or repair buildings including RFK Stadium and the White House—he was always working on *something*, whether he was building his back porch, mixing cement to pave part of his backyard, or tinkering with his car. One day when I was nine or ten I wandered into the backyard to find my father talking to Uncle Nay, who was working on something, I don't remember what. My father turned to me and said, "Look at your uncle." I looked at my uncle. Blood ran down his arm, dripping from the ends of his fingers. My father said, meaning to chide Uncle Nay but unable to keep the admiration out of his voice, "And he won't stop working!"

Uncle Nay's wife, Aunt Emma, was short and round with many tiny moles on her face—moles like the dots over New York City on a population map—and perfect teeth, not one of which, I figured out much later, was real. Aunt Emma was upright: unlike others of our relatives, she never gossiped, and the saying "waste not, want not" might have been coined with her in mind: eating dinner at her table one day, I watched her go to work on a chicken bone, which looked, when she was done, like it had been lying for two years in a desert. Emma and Nay had four daughters. (Actually, five; the first-born died at age six, which I hear nearly drove Uncle Nay crazy.) Delores had gotten married and moved to Cleveland; Emma—known since childhood as Fuzzy—had gotten married to someone named Joe and moved away but then gotten divorced and came back to her parents' house, at 234; Natlie, who owned a powder-blue Volkswagen Beetle, was soon to marry a man named Joe (who I thought for years was Fuzzy's ex-husband) and move to New York; and Vivian lived at 234, as did her two sons, Billy (almost exactly a year older than me) and Timmy (almost exactly a year younger).

My relatives would often drop by unannounced, singly or in combination, for visits of a half-hour or an hour. "Here come the crip," Aunt Emma would say, walking in with her cane; asked how she was doing, she said, every single time, "Oh, I guess I'll do." Uncle Nay might come over with a toothpick in his mouth and a stocking cap on his head. My mother would say, as she said to everyone, "Have some sit-down."

Billy, Timmy, and I, meanwhile, ran around outside, playing hide-and-seek or pointing our guns at each other or shouting "That's my bad car!" when a cool-looking set of wheels passed by. My mother liked to tell the story of when Billy and Timmy ran to my house begging her to come and "get Cliff down." She went to see what they were talking about, and what made her laugh as she told the story was how patiently I was waiting when she found me—hanging upside-down by my pants on the neighbor's fence I'd tried to climb.

Billy may have been my first hero. Strong? Once, standing in front of my house, he threw a toy pistol over the roof, and we ran around to find it in the backyard. And he started school before I did, which gave him knowledge I could barely imagine. One day on the front porch my sister Phyllis, then about fifteen, asked Billy if he could spell "up." Billy said, "U-P." I was in awe.

I remember Phyllis, my sister Wanda, and Natlie taking Billy, Timmy, and me to the movies to see *Gulliver's Travels Beyond the Moon*. That animated film, I see now, was released in 1966, which means I was three years old. I was scared out of my wits. Billy, himself all of four then, helped talk me down from my fear on the bus ride home. Another time my sisters and Natlie took us boys to Rock Creek Park, where we ran through the seemingly endless stretches of grass, charging up a hill chanting "I *think* I can I *think* I can," flying down the other side yelling "I *thought* I could I *thought* I could . . ."

Soon Natlie went off with Joe to New York, and Wanda left for college in Pennsylvania. But before all that, the sixteen of us were packed into three small houses. One incident brought all or most of us outside on our porches at once: a spectacular car crash—cars turned sideways, mangled steel, shattered glass, the whole bit—right in front of 232, 234, and 236. If I recall correctly, there was a family with a small child in one car; the other car must have been stolen, since nobody in it stuck around. Billy, Timmy, and I ran about while the adults speculated on what had happened. My brother, Wayne, then about twenty, came home to find us all outside. When someone told him what was going on, he said, "Did the cops get 'em?" I didn't know what "cops" were.

But it didn't take car crashes to bring us together. Other images live in my mind: there were the Fourth of July picnics in Aunt Catherine and Uncle Brock's long, narrow backyard, where plastic Japanese-style lanterns were strung through tree branches, glowing as the sun went down, where at age eight I had my first drink—a quarter-glass of Boone's Farm Apple Wine that later caused me to barf up my spaghetti; there was the Christmas Eve I was ten—my father's last Christmas Eve—when my parents had the other adults over, when, at midnight, long after I had been sent to bed, I was awake and looking out my window and saw Uncle Brock walk with his cane out to his car, saying something in his happy rough voice, full of holiday spirit and other spirits.

And then there was the everyday togetherness. I may not have seen my extended family on a given night, but I feel astonished, in the anonymous surroundings I've now known so long, when I think that so many of my blood relatives were once so close by, that we went to sleep and woke up within fifty feet of one another. Late at night, under the eye of a single street lamp, with the occasional whoosh of a car heading up or down Division Avenue, there we all were in our beds, dreaming, or dreading, or hoping, or planning, or remembering.

What is it about the music of the jazz pianist Thelonious Monk, which I hadn't heard then, that evokes thoughts of my older relatives? Maybe it is the wistfulness that often peeks through the surface of those spiky, dissonant melodies; maybe it is the horns in the 1947 version of "Round Midnight" that sound to me like my grandmother's tuneless humming, that bring back, say, the agreeably musty smell of the cardigans she wore even in the summertime.

===

I was born at five o'clock on a Sunday morning in the late winter of 1963. One of the earliest feelings I remember is of not having been around very long. How that can be I can't say, since you'd think that, to feel I hadn't been around long, I would've needed to be conscious in a time before my own birth; but there it is. I had that feeling on a day I recall hazily, when I was at home with Wayne, Wanda, and Phyllis, all in their teens then; I also had the sense at the time that things were shaky, because my mother, father, and grandmother weren't there. Proof that matters weren't under control was that I asked Wayne a question, and he shrugged. (I couldn't remember having seen anyone shrug before, but I got the gist.) That was probably the occasion—referred to by my family for many years afterward—when I asked for my mother, was told she'd gone out, and then said aloud, "Little boy wanted his momma, but his momma wasn't home."

Home: entering the front door of 232, you looked down a short hallway leading to our very small kitchen; you could walk down the hall, through the kitchen, and out the back door without turning once. To the right of the hallway, and parallel to it, were the wooden stairs—bare in those early days—leading to the second floor. I got acquainted with the hardness of that wood at age three, when, starting down the stairs, I thought I heard my mother call me from above and turned around to answer her; next thing I knew I was lying at the bottom, Phyllis crying and someone else kneeling beside me. (I still have the scar from the three stitches on my forehead.) To the left of the hallway was our living room, and beyond that was the center of family activity, the dining room. In the back corner of the dining room nearest the kitchen was the easy chair where my father liked to sit. Often when relaxing there, thumb under chin and index finger on bridge of nose, he watched the black-and-white TV that sat on top of a cabinet catty-cornered from his spot. Between the chair and the TV, in the center of the room, was the rectangular dining table, supported at either end by a tripod; each curved leg of the tripods was a perfect fit for my back, and I passed many an hour lying under the table, resting on the leg nearest the TV, gazing up at whatever show was on. I was there one day, watching TV, when my parents had Uncle Nay, Aunt Emma, et al., over for a gathering. As the adults enjoyed themselves and their talk got louder, a young boy's voice came from under the table: *"I CAN'T HEAR!"* Wow, did that make my mother angry.

Upstairs, at the opposite end of the hall from my parents' bedroom, was the shoebox of a room where Wayne slept, and next to that was a larger room: there, Wanda and Phyllis shared a double bed, and my grandmother shared a single bed with . . . me. That went on until my father decided that no eight-year-old boy, particularly if said boy was his son, should sleep in the same bed with his grandmother. At that point I inherited Wayne's shoebox, where Uncle Brock came to talk to me; Wayne moved to the basement, turning that into the wonderland I will discuss a bit later.

For now, I will return to my parents' room and what I believe is my very earliest memory: I am in my crib; it is dark, and the dark has a blue-ness—is it early morning? The edge of night? My parents' radio is playing instrumental music, four bars of which I remember to this day: a leisurely, happy tune with a hint of sadness.

"Sometimes I sits and thinks," goes the quote attributed to the great Satchel Paige, "and sometimes I just sits." He could've been speaking for my little-boy self. I spent a lot of time doing, well, not much—either sitting or wandering around the house, bored. If it was evening, though, I knew where I might find relief.

This brings me to my sister Phyllis.

Many, many people—I am one of them—take French in junior high or high school and then go on to forget every word they learned, if they learned any. Phyllis became fluent in French, not just because she paid attention in class but because she immersed herself in the study of the language at home in the evenings. Phyllis was a standout student at La Reine, the nearly all-white, private, Catholic high school she attended through a scholarship from our local church, St. Luke's; she had her class' highest grade-point average in her senior year, 1970, the year the school decided that the valedictory address would be given not at graduation, which all the parents would attend, but at a different function.

That thinly veiled act of racism, which I learned about many years later, did not dampen Phyllis's attitude toward her work. Phyllis, the third of our parents' four children, loved learning. She also loved spending time and sharing ideas with me—the brother, ten and a half years her junior, whose arrival made her feel hurt and jealous until, as she once told me, she decided that I would be hers. And in many ways, that is what I became. (It started with my name: she liked the actor Cliff Robertson.) When I wandered in the evenings to the room where we both slept, I would find her alone on her bed, studying (Wanda had left for college by then). I would hover in the doorway, maybe asking a question, maybe making an observation; if she was too immersed in her work to answer with anything but a monosyllable, I would quietly head somewhere else, but if she took an interest in what I was saying—oh, then we were on. It may be just as well that I haven't retained any of those conversations, since the actual words would probably detract from what I remember: wonderful, winding, soaring talks in which a young, great mind led a younger, lesser but eager one from this topic to that, like two birds flying from tree to tree, making their way across a vast city.

During those early years, my knowledge of our actual city was pretty much confined to our house. When home is all you know, frontiers are all around.

The porch of 232 was small and concrete and one step up from street level. At the edge of the porch were three waist-high brick posts topped by whitish concrete slabs that were widest at the top, like graduation caps; black metal rails, lower than the slabs, connected the posts to the house or each other. (I would sometimes straddle the left rail, gripping the sides of the slab, and pretend I was on a horse; if Billy or Timmy was on the adjacent horse, at 234, we could ride together.) To the right of our walkway was our tiny yard, with two green bushes and a third, shorter one, more blue than green, in the middle; this bush had leaves like tiny spikes, and if you fell on it with bare arms or legs, you would be sorry.

One day I stood on the porch while Billy and Timmy took off running toward Aunt Lucy, who had just shouted to us that she'd made cookies, or something. It was April 4, 1968, which I know because I later found out why my parents had forbidden me to leave the porch: there was rioting in the city. Martin Luther King had just been killed.

Another memory: a hot day when I sat at the edge of the porch, between two of the brick posts, with my feet on the walkway, drawing air into my mouth to cool off. Directly across the street was a white house on a grassy mound, and to the right of that was the frontier: the hill of Banks Place, which was perpendicular to and ended at my street. The top of the hill, as I sat at the edge of the porch, was in relief against blue sky. What was on the other side of it?

A second frontier, and another mystery, could be found behind our house. The window of our bathroom had the best view of it. Beyond the thicket of green leaves and our wooden back fence was a long, white, narrow, rough-surfaced alley; on the other side of that was a wide hill with unmowed grass, and at the top of the hill, like a red-brick mountain range, was public housing: Lincoln Heights. I often stood at the open window, feeling the summer breeze, hearing the soft, rapid clicking of cicadas, gazing at the buildings, and thinking: what goes on back there? (I was to find out, but for years my one clue raised more questions than it answered: a woman's voice of operatic power calling out once or twice a day, "Deb-or-*AH*!")

My first visit to Lincoln Heights doesn't count, because it was quick and frantic and I took in nothing. Billy and I were out back one day—I couldn't have been over five—when some boys from Lincoln Heights got into the yard; one of them snatched the blue cap from my head, and they kept going. I went in the house and told someone what had happened, and Wayne heard me from upstairs.

If I was five, Wayne was nineteen. At nineteen he was six feet tall and weighed one hundred and fifty-five pounds, the biggest thing on him being his Afro. (He could toss me around pretty well, though, and I thought he was the strongest man in the world. One day I asked Phyllis, in all serious-ness, if Wayne could beat Muhammad Ali. "Well," she began.) Wayne was generous. In those days he was the assistant manager at a dry cleaner's; he got paid every Thursday, which was a great day to be at 232: Fuzzy would come over from next door, and she, Phyllis, and I would wait for the good-ies Wayne brought home—sticky buns, cakes, pies, a couple dozen cans of soda of great variety, and other treats. My father once quipped that Wayne brought home "about thirty cents a week" after paying for all that stuff.

But for all his slenderness and generosity, you didn't want to make my brother angry. One night at the dry cleaner's a man came in with a gun and demanded the cash from the register, which Wayne gave him. Then the man made two mistakes: demanding Wayne's money, and looking away for a moment while Wayne reached in his pocket. My brother rushed the man, and they struggled for the gun. Wayne won the struggle and, as the man ran away, shot at him.

As I was saying: from the second floor Wayne heard my tearful voice, and as family lore has it, he came down the stairs two at a time. He went running toward Lincoln Heights, and Billy and I followed—through the yard, up the alley, up the grass hill and around the corner of the housing project, which felt to me like rounding the corner to the dark side of the moon. We must have been an odd sight to the residents of Lincoln Heights: three people they'd never seen before—a rail-thin, furious-looking man, trailed by a small boy, who was trailed by a smaller boy—tearing like Earth-bound comets into their neighborhood and out again. We never found the boys, but when we got back to our yard, my cap was hanging on the fence.

Wanda, born a year and a half after Wayne, was my cool, worldly sibling. She enrolled at Dickinson College, in Pennsylvania, in the fall of 1968, when I started kindergarten. In high-school photos, and in my earliest, dimmest memories of her, Wanda had straightened hair; she came back from college with an Afro worthy of the Jackson 5, and she had started smoking. (My parents smoked, but something about Wanda's doing it seemed scandal-ous. Phyllis was horrified.) I was always thrilled when Wanda came home for vacations. I always cried when she left. When she was home she always slept maddeningly late; like a pet, I would hang around the bedroom door, waiting for her to get up. When she was away I would write her letters, keeping her up to date on what passed in my life for news. Once I informed her that I had gotten a 64 pack; it was only at Phyllis's suggestion that I added "of Crayola crayons." (Sometimes my judgment slipped in the opposite direction: I once signed a birthday card to my grandmother, whose bed I shared, "Clifford Thompson." Phyllis saw that and said, "She knows who you are!") Of all of us, Wanda came the closest to getting caught up in the era's Black Power movement. Like quite a few predominantly white colleges at the time, Dickinson made an effort to recruit more blacks; when Wanda and a handful of other black students arrived on campus, no one seemed to know what to make of them. That was certainly true of the white students. Wanda endured what must have been common indignities back then ("Can I feel your hair?"); at her graduation, another student, a white woman who was all of about twenty-two, said to my fifty-year-old parents about Wanda, "You must be very proud of her." The black students, for their part, got caught up in the anti-war, anti-police, anti-white-cultural-bias, anti-you-name-it spirit of the times; their mantra was, "You're either part of the solution or part of the problem." Thus Wanda's involvement in a plan to take over the school library (a plan that seems not to have been carried out). It was all part of an idea of blackness that was as new as I felt—and that was to give me trouble down the road.

===

I found out what was beyond the hill of Banks Place: school. During those years of Lyndon Johnson's White House, I was one of his first Head Start kids, going to class in a white building with green trim that looked like a cross between a trailer and army barracks. About a hundred feet away (every inch of it concrete), on the other side of the playground equipment, was the school proper: Richardson Elementary.

In every school attended by a lot of children, there is the same smell—a mix of finger paints and crayon, playground sweat and little-kid grime. As an adult, walking into the various schools my own children attended when they were small, I always noticed the smell, and it never failed to send me, faster than the transporter on *Star Trek*, back to the feelings of my early schooldays: confusion and nervousness, excitement and yearning, with a layer, now, of pleasant sadness over what is at once visceral and irretrievable.

Low-level panic over the most mundane things is what I remember from my earliest days at Richardson. On particularly cold days, for example, I wore puffy, dark-blue snow pants, which I then spent about half the school day removing; one problem was that they were fastened partly with a large safety pin—a real misnomer, since unfastening it put me in danger of stabbing my clumsy little thumb—and by the time I negotiated all that, I was behind on something else. In those early school days I often had a hazy understanding, or none at all, of what was going on or of what I was supposed to be doing, which to this hour is probably the feeling I hate most in life. I have a clear memory of the day Mrs. Dixon, my kindergarten teacher, read from a list to tell each boy and girl how many cookies he or she had coming. Andre may have had four, Hattie six; when Mrs. Dixon got to my name, she said, "Clifford, your cookies are *out*!" Why were my cookies out, when Andre still had four and Hattie had six? What did I have to do to maintain a steady supply of cookies? If anybody had told me, it was probably while I was trying to take off my snow pants.

So imagine my surprise when I discovered, somewhere around second grade and definitely no later than third grade, that I had a reputation as the smartest boy in the class. My reputation was part illusion. I *was* smart; once I got past the snow pants and the cookies, I found that actual schoolwork came easily to me. But there were other factors at work. No small part of success in elementary school is simply doing what you're told, which was second nature to the lone small child in a household with six adult or adult-sized members. What gave my image its sheen, though, was that I sounded the part. One day in second grade, after I had read something aloud, one of my classmates said, not at all with derision (though that would come soon), "He sound like somebody on the news!" Compared with the other kids in my class, in my neighborhood, I probably did.

My neighborhood was entirely black and largely lower middle class; two housing projects—Lincoln Heights and, down the street, the Clay Terrace apartments—tilted it toward "working poor." The people who lived there weren't dumb, at least no more than in most other places; there are different kinds of knowledge and intelligence, and it seems to me now that a lot of my classmates were born knowing some things I had to learn as a grown man. It was just that the neighborhood was not, by and large, education-oriented. (Manson, Lucy, Nay, Emma, and my parents, for example, didn't have a college degree among them. When I was in about the fourth grade, my father told me I'd already had more schooling than Uncle Nay.) One day when I was in junior high school, a classmate saw me with a copy of Malcolm X's autobiography and asked, with some disdain but mostly with confusion, "Why you *read*?" Nothing in that boy's experience had led him to see reading as vital, useful, or enjoyable, and where I grew up, he was hardly alone. Other things were much more important. High on the list was who was going with whom. If there was no actual sex in elementary school (and to this day, I'm not sure), there was a lot of talk about it. I remember hearing one fourth-grade classmate of mine say to another boy about some girl, "She want me to fuck her. I'ma do it, too!" Just as important, if not more so, was who could beat whom. When the kids sensed a fistfight about to break out on the playground—a regular occurrence—a group of them would start chanting:

It's a fight! It's a fight!
'tween the nigger and the white!
Get 'im, nigger, cuz
THE WHITE CAN'T FIGHT!

Never mind that you could've searched high and low in our neighborhood without finding anything resembling a white kid.

Everybody liked a good fight. One night, in that era before cable stations, VCRs, DVD players, or streaming, when everybody watched the same thing on TV at the same time, *West Side Story* aired, and the next day all the kids talked about it at school. They seemed to have missed its message, though; there was a lot of arguing over whether the Jets had beat the Sharks or the Sharks had beat the Jets. Another time, our teacher took the class to a showing of the movie *The Learning Tree*, based on Gordon Parks's novel about growing up black in the Deep South of the early twentieth century. One sequence showed a battle royal, much like the one in Ralph Ellison's novel *Invisible Man*, in which a dozen or so black boys were thrown together in order to beat one another senseless. Maybe it was a lot to expect of elementary-school students to appreciate the significance of black boys tearing each other apart like cocks for the entertainment of the local whites; after the movie my classmates, girls included, were excited, slapping five with each other over how good the fight had been.

All of this left me feeling isolated. I didn't want to fight anybody; even if I'd been mad enough at another boy to want to hit him, which I never was, a powerful deterrent was the thought of getting hit back. As for girls, there were some I liked—I remember a girl named Rosalind—but what did you do when you "went with" one, anyway? The subject may as well have been quantum physics for all I understood about it.

Those weren't the only things isolating me. I will surprise no one by writing that people in my neighborhood spoke so-called Black English. I didn't, though. Why not? One word: Phyllis. After spending so much time listening to her, I took on a lot of her speech patterns. Why didn't she speak so-called Black English? That's anybody's guess, but mine is that her speech was influenced by the schools she attended—La Reine and, before that, Charles Young, an elementary school for gifted children.

I was like Phyllis in other ways, too. If I couldn't quite match my sister's brilliance, I had some of her enthusiasm. In third grade I would come home from school, get my homework out of the way, and then do what I really enjoyed: sit at the small rolltop desk in my little bedroom and write unassigned reports on people profiled in my Afro-American history book. US Senator Edward Brooke and W. C. Handy, "the father of the blues," were among them; so were Charles Drew, of blood plasma fame, and of course Frederick Douglass and Harriet Tubman. I loved the stories of those figures, the way they had all pulled themselves up from nothing—less than nothing, in the cases of Tubman and Douglass—and become great. The irony eluded me then—the irony that I, the one boy in my school who didn't speak Black English, was the only one spending his free time researching and writing about the lives of famous black people. I would give the finished reports, exercises in near-plagiarism, to my teacher; she always seemed a bit baffled but dutifully put them on a special table in the classroom, where they were promptly ignored. Those reports, the fact that I knew my multiplication tables forward and backward, and the solemn, all-knowing, "proper" tone with which I correctly answered questions—these all reinforced my reputation as the smartest kid. I wonder now how my classmates could stand me.

Whether or not they could stand me, they kept electing me to things. In the spring of 1974 I rode the coattails of James Brown, the Godfather of Soul, to victory. My opponents in the race for student council vice president were three other fifth-graders—the pretty tomboy Darlene Porter, my fellow egghead Inez Jordan, and the one I was really worried about, the smart but also cool Quentin Blakemore. Each of us had to give a speech at the school assembly; students were to cast their votes based on what we said. Knowing that I wasn't cool—or "bad," as we said—I decided the best strategy would be to acknowledge the problem while also trivializing it. So I invoked the name of the soul singer, who was then still a hot, able performer and not the sentimentalized relic he became before his death. "Maybe I'm not the baddest dude that ever crossed your path," I told my fellow students. "Maybe I can't sing and dance like James Brown. But I possess real leadership ability . . ." I needn't have bothered with the "leadership ability" stuff; the mere mention of the black community's hero had done the job. I collected nearly as many votes as my three opponents combined, and a year later, fond memories of the James Brown reference gave me the student council presidency, gift-wrapped. (A gift of dubious value, it must be said. Aside from giving speeches at assemblies, my main duty as vice president and president was to make sure nobody went up the down staircase when returning from lunch—an odd job for a boy who was as skinny as I was turning out to be. I did my best.)

There are a couple of ways of interpreting my election victory. One is that my identification with a black symbol—James Brown—made the kids vote for me. But if that's true, then why didn't they vote for the other kids, whose entire speeches were infused with "blackness" by virtue of the cadence of the speakers' voices? Interpretation number two is that, as much contempt as there may have been for mainstream-style speaking, there was a deeply embedded, unconscious, self-hating belief that he who had mastered it somehow deserved respect (and a vote). Yet, if that was so, why did so many kids approvingly yell "James Brown!" as they passed me in the hall?

One final stab at an explanation: it was the novelty of a reference to a black symbol, *in the context of a mainstream speech*, that excited the kids.

They saw, heard, a bit of themselves in the larger culture surrounding them.

The appeal of that approach would soon be discovered, and exploited, by TV and movie executives.

===

In about 1972, when my father retired from the Postal Service on disability, my mother started sorting mail on the night shift. Five nights a week, at exactly ten o'clock, my father drove her to the main branch of the post office in his black Dodge Coronet, his onetime taxi, whose orange stripes he had camouflaged with black paint. He returned promptly at 10:35, by which time, to his chagrin—if it was a Tuesday—he had missed half of *Barnaby Jones*. He wished aloud that *Cannon*, which aired at nine o'clock, could switch time slots with *Barnaby Jones*, which he thought the better show. This, as some will recall, was the era of the TV-detective-with-the-distinguishing-feature. Cannon was fat; Barnaby was old. (Then there was Kojak, who was bald, Longstreet, who was blind, Ironside, who was wheelchair-bound, and Columbo, who was rumpled and forgetful, but I don't recall my father's thoughts on those guys.)

I see my father in the easy chair in the corner of the dining room, chin resting on thumb, forefinger on the bridge of his nose, grinning and laughing at some TV show he would dismiss as ridiculous the second it was over. He brought that derisive fandom to quite a few programs. He watched *The Flip Wilson Show*, he watched *The Bob Newhart Show*, he watched *Dragnet*; he watched *Gunsmoke* and *Hawaii Five-O* and *The Streets of San Francisco* and *Kung Fu*, whose title he thought was the name of the main character, until Phyllis and I set him straight. "If his name is Caine," he wanted to know, "how come you got me sittin' up here lookin' at *Kung Fu*?" That was typical: *we* had him watching *Kung Fu* and all the other shows he pretended not to enjoy—otherwise, I guess, he might have been spearheading a new artistic movement or strategizing with Democratic leaders over how to win the White House. He tried to watch *The Carol Burnett Show*; he had read an article about Burnett and was impressed with how hard she worked. "But," I heard him tell Uncle Brock one day, "I just don't like her show!"

Uncle Brock sometimes played Ed McMahon to my father's Johnny Carson, a straight man and set-up artist for my father's enthusiasm over things he saw on TV. When a capsule containing a NASA astronaut splashed into the ocean within ten seconds of the ETA, my father couldn't contain himself.

"Two seconds?" Uncle Brock asked.

"*Ten* seconds," my father corrected, happy to repeat the information.

On one of the Westerns he loved, a very strong man had killed another man in a saloon brawl. "Knocked him down?" Uncle Brock later wanted to know, providing the set-up.

"Picked him up and *threw* him!" came the reply.

Television provided the background noise of my childhood; if not actively watching a show while nestled against the table leg, I glanced up at the TV while drawing comics at the dining-room table or heard it while playing on the living-room floor with my G.I. Joes. Thanks to my freakishly good memory for this kind of thing (if only I could apply it to, say, learning Italian), I still remember the ads that ran for shows before their first episodes aired. "You've got spunk," the irascible softy Lou Grant told the main character in the promo for *The Mary Tyler Moore Show*; he added, after Mary had smiled and lowered her head modestly, "I *hate* spunk!" In the ad for *M*A*S*H*, Alan Alda—dressed in army fatigues—looked into the camera and talked about the show, then said, with feigned mild surprise, "Oh, you don't know about *M*A*S*H*?"

It might not have seemed that the Moore character, Mary Richards, a single, thirtyish white woman working at a TV news station in Minneapolis, had much to say to a lower-middle-class black family in Washington, DC; her style, though, was familiar to me. When I told Phyllis once that Mary reminded me of her, she dismissed the comparison, but I knew what I was talking about: they both had an upbeat spirit and an overriding concern for others' feelings. Pistol shots at robbers and plots to take over libraries aside, my family was a polite bunch. Our running joke today is that a typical Thompson exchange begins, "What do you want to do?," to which the answer is, "It doesn't matter to me. What do *you* want to do?" With her back against the wall, Mary Richards could come out with the unvarnished truth, but until then she would go to great lengths to spare others' feelings. We Thompsons were the same way. I once purposely lost at tug-of-war because the other boy was struggling so hard I felt sorry for him. Watching Mary Richards—an

emissary from the larger culture—behave like us Thompsons fed an unconscious belief of mine, which was that once you got beyond the space aliens I
went to school with, politeness was one of the world's operating principles.
Sure, there was Rhoda, Mary's tough-talking upstairs neighbor and friend,
but she wasn't the star of the show; Mary, the one everybody adored, in part
because she was so nice, was the star of the show. How stubbornly, and
against what overwhelming evidence, my belief persisted!

"I used to hate *M*A*S*H*," I recall my father saying, his way of
making the rare admission that he liked a TV show. Whereas *Mary Tyler
Moore* was concerned with personal morals and ethics, *M*A*S*H* was
about public ones: the gifted army surgeon Hawkeye Pierce railed against
the immorality and insanity of the Korean War and, by extension, all wars.
The private conduct of Hawkeye and the other surgeons was something
else again, which may have been what my father found distasteful at first.
"Politeness" was not exactly the watchword at the 4077th Mobile Army
Surgical Hospital; Hawkeye's wit cut down friend and foe alike. Hawkeye,
his tent mate Trapper John McIntyre, and their commanding officer, Henry
Blake, drank like fish, and Trapper and Henry, who were both married, were
something less than models of fidelity—Trapper seemed to bed about as
many nurses as Hawkeye did. Like my father, I enjoyed *M*A*S*H*, even if
a lot of it went over my head. During one episode, when an aging general
made a visit to the tent of Major Margaret "Hot Lips" Houlihan—the last
visit he was ever to make anywhere—my father had to explain to me why
a nice romantic evening had killed the man. (I found out as an adult that a
jazz musician I admire, the saxophonist Benny Golson, had composed music
for *M*A*S*H*—including "Abyssinia, Henry," the episode in which Henry
is killed.)

As different as they were, what *M*A*S*H* and *Mary Tyler Moore*
both did, at least in my naïve mind, was reinforce the notion of a world
where peoples and races had once opposed one another but did so no longer—where the vast majority of people had come to realize the essential
oneness of mankind. On *Mary Tyler Moore*, the black actor John Amos—
who would soon turn up on *Good Times*—played the news station's
weatherman, who enjoyed the esteem of his colleagues. (His character even
filled in once for the vacationing anchorman, the white, dimwitted Ted Bax-

ter, and did a much better job.) Hawkeye and Trapper, who embodied the spirit of *M*A*S*H*, came across and stood up to many kinds of prejudice; the message was that any right-thinking person would do the same, were he in the rare position of coming face-to-face in the 1970s with the attitudes Hawkeye and Trapper had to deal with in 1952.

In a way, even *All in the Family*, which preceded *M*A*S*H*, *Mary Tyler Moore*, and *The Bob Newhart Show* on Saturday nights (what a lineup that was!), reinforced the notion of a new, progressive world. Yes, its main character, Archie Bunker, was a sexist bigot, but he was also the butt of the show's humor—which meant to me that everyone knew how foolish Archie's attitudes were. (I was unaware at the time of the many letters CBS received from people praising the network for finally airing a show about their kind of guy.)

There was one sitcom that went against that we-are-one-world idea—or, more accurately, against the view that the idea had prevailed. *Good Times* was a spin-off of a spin-off. The character Maude Findlay, played by Bea Arthur, had begun life on *All in the Family* as Edith's outspoken feminist cousin, a left-wing answer to Archie. Arthur was given her own show, *Maude*, on which one of the characters was Maude's maid, a black woman named Florida Evans (Esther Rolle). In 1974 Florida became one of the main characters on *Good Times*, which found Florida and her husband, James (John Amos again), living in a high-rise, low-income apartment building in Chicago's black ghetto with their three children (including, infamously, Jimmie "J.J." Walker). The often funny *Good Times* scored political points with lines that were, as the series progressed, increasingly meant to get applause from the live studio audience. (James: "Florida, Social Security's not enough to live on, it's just enough to die on"—*clap clap clap clap clap*.)

(A side note here about sitcoms filmed before live audiences. That practice, begun in the 1970s, seemed aimed at generating a theater-like feel; but of course it couldn't make watching TV feel like going to a play, and the price for that faux-theater was the absence of anything approaching subtlety. A great feature of television—the truly lifelike lines that characters spoke half under their breath—was lost when actors had to shout to be heard in the back row. How much better shows like *Happy Days* were before they started being filmed before live audiences! Shows like *The Office* have since gotten back to that quieter, more intimate and lifelike feel, with the added benefit of dispensing with the laugh track, a bizarre invention that somehow seemed natural in the 1970s.)

But to return to *Good Times*: there had been other shows with black actors and even black lead characters (*Julia* and *The Bill Cosby Show*, not to be confused with *The Cosby Show* of later years), but *Good Times* was the first network sitcom of its kind: one that focused on a poor black family. Kids in my school—me included—tuned in to *Good Times* as if trying to catch glimpses of themselves on the news. And in a way it *was* news: the larger culture had seen fit to portray people like us.

I referred earlier to a new idea of blackness. Black people were not new in the 1970s, of course, and neither were blacks' contributions to society, but the commonly acknowledged idea of blackness as something other than non-whiteness, as a thing unto itself asserted by blacks and accepted by mainstream society—*that* was new. *Good Times* was a sign of this new thing, and there were others, in many areas of life. Take, for example, the aforementioned G.I. Joes I played with on the living-room floor. In the 1960s the makers of those action figures produced black G.I. Joes by painting the white ones brown. The black G.I. Joe I owned in the 1970s, though, had a nose as wide as John Amos' and hair as rough as the stuff on the top of my own head. Then there were dashikis. (Fuzzy sewed one each for Billy and Timmy, running out of good material before she made a third one, which is why mine had flowers all over it. My mother refused to let me wear it, then relented when I kept begging her.)

The ultimate proof of the power of this new idea of blackness was that people with influence noticed it—and saw dollars signs. *Good Times* was about black people, but it was put on the air by business-minded white television executives. Black-style humor had already made it to TV in the early 1970s, with Flip Wilson's variety show and the sitcom *Sanford and Son*; after the success of *Good Times*, other sitcoms about black families were brought to the airwaves—the short-lived *That's My Mama* and the longer-lasting but wretched *What's Happening!* (which couldn't even get the punctuation in its title right).

And then there were the movies: the so-called black-exploitation or "blaxploitation" films. Most of them were rated R, but my classmates went to see them anyway, either accompanied by older relatives or let in by ticket sellers who didn't give a damn. I never went myself. My own parents and siblings did not particularly want me to see those movies, and even if they had, I probably wouldn't have gone; I was a very sensitive viewer back then, and blaxploitation flicks were nothing if not violent. So I did homework, wrote my reports on Afro-Americans, and drew comics while the kids who were "bad" went to see the likes of *Black Caesar* and *Hell Up in Harlem*—films I wouldn't see until I was an adult.

The "exploitation" label refers to Hollywood executives' taking advantage of the passions stirred up in the African-American community by the Black Power movement. Hollywood got the last laugh: most of the money spent to see a black man get even with Whitey found its way to the pockets of industry bigwigs, and guess what color *they* were. The exploitation also includes the mileage those executives got out of the stereotype of the black male as criminal. None of that seemed to matter to people in my neighborhood. The important thing was the black hero on the screen.

===

On a very hot day in June of 1969, when I was six, my cousin Natlie—then twenty-three—married Joe Allen. The wedding reception was held outdoors, at the house of some well-off relatives of my father's who lived in suburban Maryland. I remember a lot of grass. The outfit I wore, a dark blue suit with short pants, presented me with a dilemma: I thought the jacket was too cool for words, but when I wore it I was too hot for words. So I took it off, then put it back on, then took it off again, then put it on again, while my mother shook her head and Billy, age seven, walked around giving out chocolate mints. "Take two," he said with an air of authority when he got to me.

I mention all this because one of the records playing at the reception, at least according to my memory, was The Fifth Dimension's "Wedding Bell Blues." I didn't know what the singer, Marilyn McCoo, looked like, but her voice made her sound beautiful (she was); and more affectingly, she was forthright about her aching desire to marry Bill, the only man she had ever loved: "I was on your side, Bill, when you were lo-oo-sin' / I never schemed or lied, Bill, there's been no foo-oo-lin' . . ." (There really was no fooling: McCoo married her real-life husband, the musician Billy Davis Jr., the same year Natlie married Joe.) McCoo's yearning stirred that emotion in me—a nameless yearning, maybe the most powerful kind.

About a year later Phyllis came in the house and found me in a fairly representative pose—sitting back on the sofa, not doing squat. She sat down and told me she was now a counselor at a summer day camp for kids; the youngest were between first and second grades (which I was then), the oldest between fifth and sixth grades. This was the St. Luke's Summer Program, named for its location in the basement of nearby St. Luke's Church. She asked me if I wanted to attend, and after checking with my social secretary, I said, "Okay." So began my five happy summers at St. Luke's. The day was four hours, from nine to one, with reading for the first half and either arts and crafts or outdoor games after that. Once a week we went somewhere by bus, often to one of the Smithsonian museums, trips for which Phyllis and I packed the Underwood Deviled Ham sandwiches on Wonder Bread that we still talk about, one of which would probably kill me now. Maybe it was summer that made everyone more relaxed than in regular school; I remember maybe one fight in five years. Whatever the reason, we kids had a great time together. Summer! Here we need Jaki Byard on solo piano, evoking soft late-June days with tree limbs full of leaves swaying in a gentle breeze . . .

And I mention all *this* because at the end of each summer there was a talent show, which consisted mostly of kids singing hit songs while the records played in the background. The performers tended to think along the same lines: the renditions of Jean Knight's "Mr. Big Stuff" were outnumbered only by those of the Jackson 5's "The Love You Save." (I was the only weirdo singing "Raindrops Keep Falling on My Head," from *Butch Cassidy and the Sundance Kid*, followed the next summer by Johnny Horton's "Sink the Bismarck," a choice I owed to Wayne's peculiar taste in music—peculiar, anyway, for someone in northeast DC.) The Jackson 5 hit is the one that lives in my mind: eleven-year-old Michael Jackson pouring his heart and his high, perfect voice into the lines, "I'm the one who loves you / I'm the one you NEED"—this during those weeks of summer when the older girls I saw every day stirred feelings in me that I didn't know how to act on or even describe, when Michael's voice seemed to contain all the yearning I felt.

Music! I've already said that my earliest memory, from my crib, is connected to it. One day when I was in fifth grade, Wanda gave me my first

45-rpm records: "Dancing Machine" by the Jackson 5, "Payback" by James Brown, "The Lone Ranger" by Oscar Brown Jr., "Fire" by the Ohio Players, and one more I can't remember now. Then I discovered that 45s could be had for 99 cents each at the bottom of Division Avenue, in a store across the street from the bombed-out Spic and Span, and my allowance and I were off and running to buy records: "Jungle Boogie" by Kool & the Gang (probably my favorite non-jazz song to this day), "Games People Play" by the Spinners, "Nothing from Nothing" by Billy Preston, and many more.

===

Except for the wall that separated 232 and 234, Billy and Timmy may as well have been my brothers. Then, one quiet morning when I was six or seven, I couldn't find them outside. In my memory the quiet was broken only by the sound of rain, though maybe I've just seen too many movies. Either way, Billy and Timmy had disappeared—moved with their mother to an apartment elsewhere in DC. I don't remember anybody telling me beforehand, or saying anything about it afterward.

Billy and Timmy's departure broke my heart, but I wonder now whether it made me the way I am or whether, given how I already was, it was just as well in the long run that they left.

To explain what I mean, I need to mention Wayne. I've said that when I moved into my brother's old room, he went to the basement; he stayed there for two years before getting his own place, in 1973. In photos taken in our basement in the mid-1960s, some of which show me at age three or four, the rough-surfaced walls are painted yellow, the baseboards and wooden banister maroon. Several years later—during Wayne's time there—it was repainted white with a blue trim, except for the door separating Wayne's room from the laundry room. That became a sort of Berlin of basement doors, the top half the new white and blue, the bottom half the old yellow and maroon. At some point Phyllis painted white letters on the door's bottom half that read, "Wayne left me undone."

Anyhow: for the two years Wayne lived there, the basement was a funhouse for me. Over here were the model cars Wayne had so carefully assembled, and next to those were the spray cans he used to paint the cars' various parts; over there were Wayne's tens of thousands of baseball cards, which for a time inspired a collection of my own; over that way were the record albums Wayne, Wanda, and Phyllis had bought over the years; and over this way were Wayne's *Archie* and *Superman* comic books and volumes of reprinted *Peanuts* and *Dick Tracy* comic strips. These last items set me on the path I would follow the rest of my childhood, the one I'm probably still on.

I read all those *Peanuts* books, by the great Charles M. Schulz, and then I re-read them, and then I read them some more. The kinship I felt with Charlie Brown went a long way toward explaining my love of the strip. Charlie Brown was a loser, in both the original sense of the word—he simply lost in a lot of situations—and the modern sense: he seemed to have inherent qualities that made life more difficult for him than it was for other people. But those qualities did not prevent readers from seeing themselves in him, since they often seemed to amount to no more than bad luck—and who wouldn't rather blame his failures on his luck than on himself? (The fault, dear Snoopy, lies not in our selves . . .) True, his falling—literally—for Lucy's offers to hold the football while he ran to kick it, despite her having tricked him innumerable times in the past, suggested a trust that bordered on stupidity; but is trusting people the worst sin there is? True, the baseball team of which Charlie Brown was pitcher and manager was routinely slaughtered; but that was hardly his fault alone, even if he did always shoulder the blame. Unlike, say, Lucy, he at least knew there was a game in progress. (Charlie Brown's being the team manager, which I found puzzling as a boy, now makes perfect sense to me. Managing people, as I have since found out, is an inexhaustible source of headaches, and who would be more likely to find himself in that role?)

There were a couple of differences between Charlie Brown and me. One was skin color. The other was that Charlie Brown experienced things that, most of the time at least, I feared rather than suffered. But the first difference was unimportant to me, and I wasn't even aware of the second, because, as I realize now, the thought of suffering Charlie Brown–like experiences was as big a drag as the experiences themselves. In those days I had a mortal fear of being laughed at, and my school life was filled with events designed, it seemed to me, to bring about that result. I hated the tumbles we were made to do in gym class; I was afraid of doing them wrong, not because I might snap my scrawny neck but because there was a roomful of kids ready to laugh at any mistake. There were sometimes dances in the auditorium during school hours, and I would rather have lost a toe than set one on the dance floor. When other kids laughed at Charlie Brown, he seemed like my fellow soldier, taking a bullet that could just as easily have hit me.

I also found *Peanuts* uproariously funny. I often ran to read the strips to my parents and siblings, sometimes barely able to get the words out because I was laughing so hard. One strip struck me, when I was in second grade, as the height of sophistication and wit. In it, Charlie Brown and Linus stand at the wall where they often hang out together; Linus tries to assure Charlie Brown that he is not alone in having places where he doesn't feel he fits in, and asks if any place in particular makes him uncomfortable. In the last panel, Charlie Brown replies, "Earth!"

So here is what I meant about Billy and Timmy's departure: I wonder if, had they continued living next door to me, we would have grown apart anyway, given the solitary habits I was developing. In what is now called imaginative play, I found I preferred being alone; the whole point, to me, was to use my own imagination, not to collaborate with some kid who was too dumb to know what I was talking about. That was true when I played with my G.I. Joes, and it was true when it came to that time-honored creative outlet of the loner: drawing comics.

My love of Charlie Brown inspired me to create my own strip, "Jerome," which was basically *Peanuts*, except that it was not drawn particularly well, even by the standards applied to eight-year-olds, and it wasn't very funny—I looked at the strips again several years later, and even I didn't get the jokes. (There was one exception: I drew a strip in which a girl, sad that her dress has shrunk in the washing machine, decides to get in the machine herself. Sometime afterward Carl Anderson, the cartoonist who drew *Henry,* had the exact same idea.) Schulz's *Peanuts* collections—whose titles included *Very Funny, Charlie Brown!* and *You've Had It, Charlie Brown!*—sometimes had lines on their covers that read, for example, "Selected Cartoons from *You're Out of Your Mind, Charlie Brown!*" Making my own, stapled "Jerome" books, I imitated the "selected cartoons from" practice, which meant I had to draw some of the cartoons twice.

Later, owing to the *Dick Tracy* strips and the many TV detective shows I watched and loved (even when I couldn't always follow their plots), I drew a cartoon series about a cop I named Jackson Ross. And then there were superheroes. Wayne was a fan of DC Comics (home of Superman and Batman); I read all those, then started walking to the drugstore at the bottom of Division Avenue with my allowance for books of my own. The drugstore carried mostly Marvel Comics, so those were what I bought—*Spider-Man*, *The Incredible Hulk, The Avengers, Thor, The Fantastic Four*. I found the Marvel books intriguing for the same reasons I found them frustrating. Whereas Superman and Batman stories were self-contained, the Marvel books were serials, which made reading one of them like walking into a good movie half an hour late and then leaving during the climax. The stories were frequently self-referential; also, maybe because they all somehow lived in New York, the costumed heroes were always wandering into one another's magazines and, often as not, fighting each other—Daredevil duked it out with Captain America, the Thing of the Fantastic Four traded blows (foolishly) with the Hulk, Spider-Man took on the X-Men. All you needed to make sense of a *Superman* comic book was third-grade reading comprehension, but with Marvel I got the sense of a vast, fascinating, endlessly interconnected world that I was clueless about and, partly for that reason, couldn't wait to explore. (I would feel much the same when, as an adult, I first listened to jazz with both ears.)

While I explored, I drew superhero comics of my own. My first hero was designed to instill terror in the heart of the criminal element: wearing an all-yellow costume, he was called . . . the Canary. Later came Blockbuster and Captain Cogent, the latter named with the help of a Thesaurus (I had looked under "powerful"). I was no prodigy; the comics I made in elementary school were terrible, the stories as ludicrous as the drawings were laughable. ("Pretty tired lion," my father said, sounding a little tired himself, after reading a story in which the Canary saved the populace by tying the tail of an escaped lion to a street sign.) But I didn't know how terrible my stuff was, which is why I was able to keep at it until I got better. And in the meantime I had found what made me happy, which was creating things alone. It gave me what I often lacked, as the only kid in the house, as the only kid like me at school, as one who lived in a world where beloved cousins could move away with no warning: control.

During the cold months of the 1971–72 school year, when I was in third grade, my father brought home a cat that somebody he knew didn't want or couldn't keep. My family was soon to make the connection between animal hair—particularly cat hair—and my periodic bouts of asthma; but that hadn't happened yet, which was why, on the day I am recalling, I was home from school, propped up in my parents' bed and struggling for breath. For part of the day I was alone with my grandmother, who was seventy-seven or seventy-eight and who could hear what you said only if you stood right beside her and spoke as if to someone a block away. At one point, while she was doing laundry or something in the basement, my breathing went from bad to worse—my lungs, which already felt as if they had shrunk to the size of thimbles, seemed to be shutting down altogether. I shouted for my grandmother, but she couldn't hear me. Then my parents walked in, took one look at me, and whisked me off to the hospital. I came home that evening, my breathing restored (I never saw the cat again), and returned to my parents' bed. Beside me was a stack of Wayne's *Peanuts* books; I was comfortable after a day of misery; and there was no place I had to go. It was the happiest moment of my childhood.

===

It may come as a relief at this point to hear that I had friends as a boy. I met two of them during my last year at the Summer Program, and in that way I explored another frontier: they lived in Lincoln Heights. I had already met boys from there at Richardson Elementary, but the ones who made an impression on me—as is often the way—did so for the wrong reasons: their hair was dull and uncombed, and they had a smell that was just this side of bad, a mix of earth and sweat that always made me think of chocolate gone wrong. (To be fair, I used to smell that way myself sometimes.) My new friends, though, were different.

Dana West was handsome. His coloring was just short of light, and he had brown hair that was always cut short. He was wiry and not very tall for his age, but since he was two and a half years older than me, and since I wasn't so tall for my age either, I looked up to him in both senses of the term. Dana was a friendly boy, which was what first drew me to him. He also had what it took to be "bad" in Lincoln Heights—he knew how to fight, jone, and fuck. (More on joning later.) The string that tied the whole Dana West package together was his gift for gab. In his long, beautiful stretches of talk he didn't feel the need to know the definitions of all the words and phrases he used, or even, necessarily, to know what he was talking about. Once, when we were playing basketball, I saw him make an improbable hook shot, which he referred to for a long time afterward as "the turn of the century." Another time, he told me that because the astrological sign of a mutual friend of ours was Cancer, the crab, it was in our friend's nature to pick at people, like a crab using pincers—to make fun of people, to "deviate" them. Did Dana mean "defame"? "Deride"? Neither: he liked the way "deviate" sounded and thought it was worthy of meaning what he wanted to say.

I loved listening to him. And for some reason, Dana liked me—*me!*, the skinny, proper-talking egghead who modeled his behavior on his sister's. Maybe I was a novelty; maybe he just thought I was nice. Whatever he saw in me, he talked so long that he hit on things he must not have talked about with his friends in Lincoln Heights; it once got back to me that Dana had called me his "only real friend."

Big Darryl—our deviating Cancer friend—was different. I looked up to Dana; Big Darryl, tall, brown-skinned, and nearly as thin as me, I simply liked a lot. We appreciated each other's dry sense of humor. He once told me about myself, "You have to know you a long time to know you." Darryl had a touch of the mainstream about him, too—he just hid it better than I did. With him it was more a matter of tastes than speech. He was the only boy in our neighborhood who watched tennis. Instead of WOL or WOOK, the soul radio stations in DC, he listened to the rock station, WPGC; Darryl said that by the time the rock hits (like KC and the Sunshine Band's "That's the Way I Like It") made it to the soul stations, where they were discovered by the rest of Lincoln Heights, he was already sick of them.

Through Dana and Big Darryl I met a third friend. Little Darryl was pudgy and affable. (He was called Little Darryl because he was shorter and a year younger than Big Darryl, but he was also called Fat Darryl, while Big Darryl was alternately called Skinny Darryl. Then there was Big Darryl's cousin Sports Darryl, also known as All-Pro Darryl—but never mind about him.) I didn't like Little Darryl as well as I did Dana and Big Darryl, but I enjoyed his company well enough, and since he was Dana and Big Darryl's buddy, I hung out with the three of them, singly and together.

Once I knew Dana and the Darryls, I got to see Lincoln Heights—also known in the neighborhood as Simple City—up close. Its three buildings formed an L, with a playground and grassless lot nestled in the corner. Each building was three stories high, with two apartments on each floor. None of the buildings had a front door. Walking through one of the building's doorways brought an assault on the senses. It was always dark, so that you held the iron rail as you felt your way up concrete steps; the first floor sometimes smelled of stale urine, and as you went higher, cooking smells took hold of your nose. The insides of the apartments were small but nice. The two Darryls each had a bigger bedroom than I did (then again, neither had a basement). Each apartment had wall-to-wall carpeting exactly like the fringe on a winter scarf, and the living-room sofas and easy chairs had that peculiar feature of furniture in lower-middle-class black homes (including, later, ours): it was covered in clear plastic.

And I met Deborah! She was a girl a little younger than me, whose mother seemed to marry frequently. The woman who bellowed her name daily was her very fat grandmother.

In the beginning Dana and the Darryls treated me, the private-home innocent, more gently than they treated each other, acted toward me with that combination of reverence and condescension some people fall into around priests. (I guess I didn't help matters by becoming the chaplain of the Boy Scout troop we all joined.) While I appreciated that to a degree, it also made me a little uncomfortable. So I was relieved when, one day, after I had made a snooty-sounding comment that began with the word "Suppose," Dana said to me calmly, "*Suppose* you suck my dick, you doin' all this supposin'?"

There seemed to be a rule about fathers in our neighborhood. Boys on Division Avenue and points farther east had them; boys west of Division Avenue—i.e., those in Simple City—did not. Dana told me once that his father had died in a car accident. Big Darryl's father left the family when the children were very young. I never found out about Little Darryl's father. During one of our serious moments together, Dana asked me, "What's it like to have a father?" I don't remember my answer.

What did Dana, the Darryls, and I do together? Sometimes, when my friends and I stayed inside, we played board games—Monopoly, Sorry!, or Life. But mostly we were outside. Someone had cut the bottom out of a milk crate and attached the rest, with wire hangers, to the top of the slide in the Lincoln Heights playground; that was our basketball hoop. I am the world's worst basketball player, but in those days I played so often that I rose to mediocrity. The playground had a swing set that was, for reasons unexplained, missing its swings; I brought badminton racquets and shuttlecocks I'd found in my family's basement to Lincoln Heights, where the frame of the swing set became our net. (Big Darryl, the tennis fan, kept us informed of which famous player each of us was.) Sometimes we played touch football in the loooong, skinny alley that separated the backyard of 232 from Lincoln Heights. Other times, we hung out and talked on the cement Lincoln Heights balcony that overlooked the alley and my backyard; leaning over the balcony's rail, looking down ten feet to the top of the hill, we could see dozens of rats, crawling over one another.

Dana and I spent a lot of time with our slingshots. My father had shown me how to make one by sawing off a Y-shaped section of tree limb and shaving the bark off with a pocket knife; the patch that held the rock could come from an old shoe. But whereas my father had connected the patch to the slingshot frame with rubber from an old inner tube, Dana showed me how to do it with rubber bands, which launched the rocks a lot farther and at much greater speed. We shot mainly at tin cans, but I got so I could hit just about anything. One day, standing on my back porch, I saw a bird in Uncle Manson's tree, two backyards away. I shot at it mostly because I thought I couldn't hit it—then watched in amazement and horror as the bird fell, squawking and spiraling, to its death.

Then there was joning, or trading insults. This, of course, has a long tradition in the black community; sometimes it's called "playing the dozens" or "signifying." I've forgotten what started one particular joning session between me and Little Darryl in his bedroom, but he ended it with two words. This was one of those somebody-finally-said-what-everybody-was-thinking moments; the laughter from the other boys would have drowned out any response I made, which was just as well, since no comeback was possible.

The two words, of course, were "white boy."

I wasn't the only one at 232 who had made new friends.

On the night of Thanksgiving 1973, when I was in fifth grade, there came into our lives—like a character introduced in the second act of a play to show the others in a new light—a twenty-eight-year-old, Nigerian-born graduate student in public health. Phyllis, who was then twenty-one, announced that this person, whom she had met at church, was coming over in the evening, after we had all stuffed ourselves with turkey. As her visitor's arrival got closer, Phyllis became anxious—about the visit as a whole, no doubt, but particularly about one problem: she couldn't remember his name. Darkness came (I remember that *Hello, Dolly* was on TV), the doorbell rang, Phyllis went to answer it, and my mother went to her rescue. As soon as the impeccably mannered guest walked in, Ma said, "It's so nice to meet you. Please tell me again: what is your name?" Phyllis cocked an ear. Our smiling visitor said, "Odun."

Well, yes and no. The pronunciation of the vowel in "Odun," situated somewhere between a short and long "u," turned out to be a target that most people we knew couldn't hit, though many shots were fired. For some, the second syllable of my future brother-in-law's name rhymed with "gun"; one woman Phyllis knew called him "Odew." Finally Phyllis and Odun agreed that everyone should call him by his Anglicized name, which was Elliot.

I didn't know what to make of this Elliot—not the name, but the man, and his place in my sister's life. I was often hanging around the living room or dining room when he came over, and so I witnessed the first stages of their relationship. In those days Elliot's affection often took the form of teasing and playfulness, much of it physical, which made Phyllis laugh in a way I'd never heard before; no doubt part of me was jealous, but I also didn't know whether she was enjoying herself or being tortured, and the uncertainty made me uncomfortable. Another thing I didn't know was that my feelings were written all over my face—until the day Phyllis said to Elliot in my presence, "Have you seen the way Cliff looks at you when you do that?"

What's clear in retrospect is that Phyllis was falling in love, and Elliot had already fallen. One night the three of us went in Elliot's long purple car to McDonald's; Phyllis went inside to order, leaving Elliot and me in the parking lot, and at one point I went in to ask or tell Phyllis something, then went back to the car. Elliot asked me, "Does she look happy?"

If I was uncomfortable, my father was amused. One day I was on the front porch with him and either Uncle Nay or Uncle Brock when Phyllis and Elliot pulled up across the street. They took a long time to get out of the car, and my father laughed with my uncle over how they were "smooching," as Daddy put it. One day not long after he had begun seeing Phyllis, Elliot wrote her a letter full of his feelings, which he sent via airmail, whose pomp must have seemed to him to fit the occasion. My father, the old Post Office hand, said with equal parts amusement and sympathy that it would have arrived sooner with a regular old stamp. There is a photograph somewhere of Elliot and my father, sitting at our dining room table; my father is smiling, Elliot looking at him admiringly.

Then there was Grandma. One night I went upstairs to bed, leaving Phyllis and Elliot downstairs. On the way to my room I passed Grandma's, where she was sitting at the window with a view of Elliot's car. I heard her say, talking to herself in that voice that was so loud because she couldn't hear it, "Why don't he go home!"

===

Grandma was born Maggie Floretta Vaughan in 1894 in the tiny town of Massie's Mill, Virginia. She was one of eight children of Sally Chew and her third husband, Shafer Vaughan, who was half white. "He was a good man," my grandmother told me several times over the years about her father; she always added, with a look of bewilderment unchanged by the passage of time, "but he was *cruel*." Her stories about him illustrated both points, especially the second. One day he hit her hard enough to raise a lump on her head that was still there when I was born, about six decades later. But in his last moments he told his wife about their sickly daughter, "Make sure Maggie sleeps by the fire."

Maggie became a schoolteacher. She told me that one day in 1912 she left the school and drove her horse and buggy home, where she heard the news that the *Titanic* had sunk.

She married Robert Ligon, a blacksmith, who served in World War I. After the war they had two children: a son, Fairfax, born in 1919, followed five years later by a daughter, Juanita—my mother. The four of them lived on a hilltop in a wooden house that rocked so badly in the wind that they had to sit in their car during storms. They raised chickens, owned a hog, and grew apples and peaches in their yard that Maggie cut up and sealed in jars that were kept in a closet; the hog got cut up, too, and put in an ice box at the end of the porch. The outhouse was the equivalent of half a block from where the family lived; twice a day they took a tin half a mile to a stream where they got water for drinking and washing.

In the 1940s, finding little to do in Massie's Mill, Fairfax and Juanita moved to Washington, where Juanita lived for a time with Uncle Manson and Aunt Lucy. She had a dizzying series of jobs, including domestic worker, waitress, and Western Union messenger. During those war years, she said, she hated delivering telegrams with black borders; those were the ones informing people that their sons or husbands had been killed.

Juanita often went to hear music, seeing the likes of Duke Ellington, Erroll Garner, and Count Basie at the Howard Theater (which she pronounced thee-AY-ter). Her social circle came to include a young man who, like her, had made his way from rural Virginia to DC: William H. Thompson, whom everyone called Dean—my father.

Dean was born on New Year's Day 1921 in Massie's Mill, the eighth of Bland and Susie Thompson's eleven kids. (Yes, Bland—a name that got passed on to a son and then a grandson, one of Uncle Brock and Aunt Catherine's two boys. Luckily for him, he was called Buddy.) Granddaddy Bland was a poor dirt farmer. When Dean was three the Thompsons moved to Arrington, Virginia, and then in 1934 they moved again, to Washington, where Susie supported her children for years as a domestic worker and where the family enjoyed things they hadn't had before—running water, flushing toilets, and electricity. Six of the Thompson children, including Dean, entered the DC public schools. Because of the perceived difference between city and rural education, Dean repeated several grades, graduating from Armstrong High School at age twenty-one. He was his class's valedictorian. My Uncle Harry, Dean's younger brother, told me in 2008 that he looked up to my father, who "always had the right answer to things." The two of them did church work together. After high school Dean worked at the Hot Shoppes before getting the job of valet to Cordell Hull, the US secretary of state under President Franklin Roosevelt. He was in that job when he was drafted. He served as a staff sergeant in the Aleutian Islands during World War II, an experience that "changed him," Uncle Harry told me. After his return he didn't attend church. He had found a different pastime: gambling. He and Uncle Harry grew apart as Dean began spending time drinking and playing cards at Uncle Manson's house, along with Manson's brother Jimmy, Uncle Nay, Nay's half-brothers Curtis and Leroy, and others. The gambling went on throughout my childhood, though I was a grown man before I realized the extent and the cost of it. My mother and siblings weren't so lucky.

Dean and Juanita married in early December 1946. My siblings came along later in the 1940s (my brother) and early 1950s (my sisters). Meanwhile, also in the late 1940s, Granddaddy Robert had passed away, and a short time later Maggie came to DC to live with Juanita, her new husband, and their children, for whom she became a live-in babysitter. By then, as I see from old photos, my grandmother had for the most part taken on the physical appearance she would have for the rest of her unusually long life: slender limbs, low-slung bosom, white and iron-gray hair tied back in a bun. The biggest change to come was in her hearing, which had—ironically, given the size of her ears—all but disappeared in my first memories of her. I don't know exactly when she lost her teeth, though those, too, were gone by my early childhood. When she went out she would put in the bottom plate of her dentures; something had happened to the top plate.

It was my grandmother's presence in our household that defined for me what our family was about. Grandma, who was old and all but deaf and couldn't be left alone for very long, was the person in the house around whom everything had to be planned; if we all wanted to go out, the first question was, "Who's going to stay with Grandma?" Nobody minded, or seemed to mind, and so it didn't occur to me that somebody might. I was grown before I heard Ma complain about it and heard that my father had griped to my poor mother on the subject. When I was a boy it seemed to me that we took care of Grandma uncomplainingly because that was what people who loved each other did. And we loved Grandma dearly—Grandma, who sewed me a coonskin cap like the one Daniel Boone wore on the TV show, who even sewed clothes for my G.I. Joes. She couldn't hear most of what we were saying and usually didn't know what was going on with us. (A frequent exchange, after I had said something to her, went as follows. Grandma: "Yeah." Me: "What'd I say?" Grandma: "I don't know.") Her lack of knowledge of the particulars meant that she went on faith, that she loved and trusted us no matter what, and that to me was the wonderful thing about her. Her love often, very often, took the form of worry. In later years, when I came home late from one place or another, she would say, seated in the armchair by her window, "I thought somebody had done knocked ya in the head," or, "I had every thought." She was once heard to say, I believe truthfully, "I spent half my life waiting and the other half being scared."

If her love for us took the form of worry, mine assumed a different shape. One day as a teenager I discovered, in the basement, a paperback copy of a biography of Gandhi; the cover illustration showed the great man's tan skin, huge ears, and lack of teeth and hair—a dead ringer, baldness aside, for my grandmother. I used to have great fun showing her the cover and shouting, "Look, Grandma, it's you!" She would shake her fist at me and look angry, though she wasn't. To communicate with her, in addition to writing notes, I would sometimes speak into one end of an old wrapping-paper roll—which I christened the Grandmaphone—while holding the other end to her ear. She bore it stoically when I made her dance with me; our rather slow version of the tango included, at my direction, a simultaneous kick at the end.

Dean worked for the railroad before becoming a clerk typist for the Postal Service, the job he had for the rest of his working life. (He had learned to type in the army.) During the first half of my elementary-school years, he would pull up in the old black Dodge Coronet every day at five-thirty. Then my mother started full-time night work; my father retired, when he was about fifty-two and I was about ten; and the period encompassing my clearest memories of him began.

As a small boy I had thought my father was fat, a perception that doesn't stand up to old photographs. Standing around five-foot-ten, he was a normal-sized, even slender man; what confused me, probably, was being at eye level with his middle-aged-dad's stomach, a modest bulge in the short-sleeved, solid-colored, button-down shirts he liked to wear. I remember those shirts, a light green one in particular; I remember straight-legged pants and wing-tip shoes. If he ever wore anything else, I've forgotten it. He had close-cropped hair, my father, and a high forehead, the kind people associate with intelligence. He wore a bridge where his original front teeth had gone missing. He was fairly light-skinned for a black man, lighter than I am—which has always seemed curious to me, since my mother was, too. I know I'm not adopted, though; for years my siblings have been telling me how much I look like my father, particularly when I smile, and lately even I've been able to see what they're talking about.

Dean's early retirement had to do with heart and gastrointestinal troubles. He drank Maalox the way other people drink water, and he always carried with him a round metal pillbox of tiny nitroglycerin tablets; his most frequent gesture was a kind of reverse-motion Aryan salute in which he gently pounded his stomach and chest to relieve pain and pressure. He was hospitalized for several days when I was in third grade. The program for Dean's funeral noted that he "bore his suffering comparably to Job," and it's true that I don't remember him once complaining about his ailments.

I do recall his irritation at a host of other things, which makes more sense to me now than it did then. He wasn't working; my grandmother couldn't hear; my mother slept during the day so she could work at night; Wayne had moved out; Wanda was now a grad student in psychology at Temple University, in Philadelphia; and Phyllis, though she remained at home, was busy with her studies at local George Washington University. For company my father often had me, at a time when he was frequently in pain and I was a preadolescent boy—by definition a person who does idiotic things for no reason he can name. Looking back, I can appreciate the restraint he often showed; at the time, not knowing how sick he was, I picked up only on his irritation, and I sometimes felt nervous around him. One day he asked me, with a snarl in his voice, why I had removed the plastic strip from the rim of a pack of the cigarettes he couldn't keep from smoking; the real answer was, *It was there and I'm ten years old*, but how could I have said that, or even thought it? I don't remember what nonsense I mumbled instead. Another time we were alone at the dining-room table, he reading the *Washington Post*, I, well, being ten, which at that moment involved playing with a yo-yo shaped and painted to look like a basketball. Why did

I put the yo-yo's finger loop over the handle of the spoon sticking out of the sugar dish? No particular reason, I guess, since I soon forgot I had done it. I wouldn't remember today, except that the yo-yo rolled off the table, pulling the spoon with it, capsizing the top of the dish, and causing a sugar rainstorm all over the table. My father looked up a moment, said something wearily under his breath that I was lucky enough not to catch, then went back to the *Post*.

Not all of our interactions were like that. We played a lot of games: Scrabble (that was big in our house), checkers, chess. He beat me in every checker game—except one, near the end of which, so conditioned by defeat that I didn't believe my own eyes, I hesitated to make the winning move. When I looked at him, as if to ask, *Is this really happening?*, he was smiling, encouraging me to victory. (Did he let me win? Possibly.) We were more evenly matched at chess, which Wanda had learned in college and taught me, Phyllis, and my father; a few of my wins, though, may have owed something to Dean's aging eyes—when we played on my small magnetic travel set, he complained that he couldn't tell the pieces apart.

How did he occupy himself mainly? Different ways. He did jobs around the house, like painting the front-porch glider and the back-porch stairs. He fixed dinner. Phyllis and I still laugh about those dinners—seven-course meals in which the courses were all served at once and consisted largely of leftovers: a glass bowl of seven lima beans over here, one with thirteen kernels of corn over there, one with two spoonfuls of apple sauce next to that. He went to the racetrack; he took me with him once. He read the *Post* from front to back. His appreciation for the newspaper and the written word led him one day to type up the front page of a mock paper. The part I remember best—the weather report in one of the upper corners—gives an idea of his sense of humor: "Chance of rain today ten percent. Maybe yes, maybe no." Sometimes, I think, he just didn't know what to do. That's the only explanation I can think of for the time he gathered up several of Wayne's cans of spray paint and went outside to where his car was parked. By the time he came back in, the car looked like the inside of a New York City subway train, circa 1978. (It didn't stay that way for long; my mother, who had to ride to work in it, saw to that.)

And one thing he did in the midst of all that, as I now understand, was think about me. I'll never know for sure what his thoughts were, but I can guess some of them. He saw me as a smart and otherwise normal boy who spent maybe a little too much time around his older sister (I know for a fact he was happy about my friendship with Dana); he saw himself as a father with one foot in the grave who had been remiss in his duty, who needed to show his son how to be a man—for that matter, how to be a boy—before it was too late.

So here we are, in the backyard, with my newly purchased baseball and gloves, throwing and catching. It is during these sessions—and there are many—that my father's restraint breaks down. He throws the ball to me; I raise my glove hand to catch it, my other hand involuntarily rising along with it; my father yells at me to keep my other hand down if I don't want him to call me a girl. I miss a catch, prompting him to tell me that I'll be sixteen before I'm good enough to play Little League baseball. Wincing from the exertion, in that way of his that shows his teeth, he pounds his stomach or reaches for his pillbox; meanwhile, I seethe with hurt and anger that I don't know how to, or am afraid to, express.

On Monday, November 11, 1974, not long before my school day would've ended anyway, another sixth-grader notified me that there was a man waiting for me in the school office. I went downstairs, only to be told that the man had gone upstairs looking for me. When I got back to my classroom, the man turned out to be Wayne, looking as serious as I'd ever seen him. Instead of hello, he said, "Get your things together." Out in the hall, I said, "What's going on?"

He told me, with no preamble, "Daddy's dead, Cliff."

I didn't say anything or react in any way. The first thing that came to my mind was the image of a dagger. That tells me, now, how little I understood about my father's health. If Daddy was dead, which is what Wayne seemed to be saying, surely it was because of some violent, unnatural act, like a stabbing. I'd just seen him the night before!

We walked over the hill of Banks Place, toward home—Wayne did, anyway. Gripping my arm, otherwise seeming to forget I was there, my tall, brokenhearted brother dragged me along like a pull toy. At 232, in an attitude of strange calm, were Ma, Grandma, and Wanda, who was visiting and was supposed to have returned to grad school the day before—but who had gotten strep throat, an illness that seemed to slip out the door in all the confusion. Also there were the first of the friends and relatives who would fill our house for the next week. Phyllis was on her way home from Princeton, where she had started grad school in religion two months earlier. I don't remember what anyone said to me; I remember only a long, silent hug with Grandma.

I felt—nothing. That seemed wrong, but there it was. I went for a walk up the alley. I think my family thought I was trying to walk off my emotions; I was trying to hide because I didn't have any. Wayne came after me, and we went up the alley together, quietly. We turned left, then left again, and soon we were coming down Division Avenue. We ran into a middle-aged neighbor who had heard about my father and started talking to us about life's disappointments. I wanted a big stick to hit her with. Wayne and I continued home, and I went up to my room. That didn't work, either; soon Ma called up the steps to tell me my friends were here. I went back down.

I don't remember how Dana, Big Darryl, and Little Darryl had heard, but there they were. Coats open, mouths closed. They didn't know what to say, or maybe they knew there was nothing to say.

But I said something. Maybe there's an excuse for what came out of my mouth that day, not two hours after my father's death. Maybe it could be blamed on the fact that I was eleven years old. Or that I felt pressured to respond to what had happened. Maybe I had an overdeveloped sense of drama from watching too much TV. Maybe I wanted to be like my fatherless friends.

I looked at Dana. "Remember when you asked me what it was like to have a father?"

"Yeah," he said.

Solemnly: "I don't know no more."

In my memory the events of the days that followed are as jumbled-up, as blurry here and vivid there, as events in a dream. The backdrop to the dream was the crowd of people, inescapable people, who filled every part of the house at every minute of the day: Manson and Lucy, Catherine and Brock, and Emma and Nay were there, of course; so was Nay's half-sister Ginny, Dean's brother Bob, Bob's wife, Bessie, their son, Billy, and many, many more, bringing food and producing a conversational buzz, continuous like the hum of an air conditioner. A few things stand out from the buzz: Elliot showing up with tears in his eyes; a woman I didn't recognize crying hysterically and being comforted by, of all people, my mother; Aunt Bessie later performing the same service when my mother herself broke down. Someone's cigarette burned a small black crater in the tan, imitation-leather dining-table top my parents had bought the previous week; the tabletop and its scar stayed there for the rest of my childhood and for years after that.

When I found time to myself that week, I thought hard about my father. It seemed to me monstrous to feel as little as I did, to be unable to cry; I wanted to trigger something in myself, to have my father's death hit me the way it should and finally set my grief in motion. I failed. It couldn't have helped that a small part of me was taken with the idea—something between a feeling and a fantasy—that my father wasn't really dead. He had actually gone somewhere else to do something different, something very important and therefore secret. Why else would he have been walking around one day and gone the next? That idea wasn't wholly dispelled even when I saw him in his casket, looking exactly as he had in life. (His corpse's resemblance to his living self gave me expectations about other funeral-home viewings, expectations that have yet to be met.) I touched his hand, which felt like it had been refrigerated. And I remember one moment from the funeral: when, at the gravesite, a uniformed military man began playing "Taps" and I looked sideways at my mother, who had her head down, eyes and lips shut tight, weeping hard and without a sound.

Interlude

For all the differences in the paths that Wayne, Wanda, Phyllis, and I have taken in our lives, there are things we still have in common—one being our love of the first two *Godfather* films. I am one of those annoying people who can think of a *Godfather* quote for any occasion or cite a scene from the films analogous to any given circumstance in life. I've lost count of how many times I've seen each film, and I don't remember when I first saw either in its entirety, but I know the first time I saw *The Godfather* at all: on TV late at night during the week my father died. It may, in fact, have been the same day.

In the movie, whose action begins in the mid-1940s, the New York mobster Vito Corleone (played by Marlon Brando) is gunned down by the henchmen of a heroin dealer; the dealer needs Vito—who wants no part of the heroin trade—out of the way so he can deal directly with Vito's son Santino (James Caan), who he senses is willing to give protection and financing in return for profit from drug sales. The attack on Vito fails, though just barely; the don lies in the hospital while Santino—Sonny—confers with other members of the crime family. Should Sonny have the dealer murdered, as he is itching to do? Or, if Vito dies, should he go into the very lucrative heroin business with the dealer, as the family consigliere (Robert Duvall) urges?

What is the right response to what has happened to his father?

To everyone's surprise and initial amusement, Vito's youngest son—the up-to-now straight-arrow Michael (Al Pacino)—proposes a plan. Over dinner in a restaurant, Michael will meet with the heroin dealer and the dealer's crooked-cop bodyguard, ostensibly to hear the terms of the business proposition. During dinner Michael will politely excuse himself and go to the men's room, where he will find the pistol that has been planted for him, then come out and shoot the dealer and bodyguard to death. Sonny and the others, once they stop laughing, go for Michael's plan.

The scene I remember watching, from my old spot against the table leg, is the one in which Michael enters the men's room. There is a roar—the sound of the subway rumbling through below; having never been to New York or ridden any subway, I took the roar to be the turbulence in Michael's head. (And, of course, I wasn't wrong.) Michael goes into a stall and searches anxiously for the gun; more unnervingly still, he finds it. He pockets the gun and returns to the table, where, as the drug dealer talks, Michael's face grows more and more tense—until, at last, he rises and shoots each of his dinner companions in the head. As instructed, he drops the gun and heads for the door.

His father may be dead; he's not completely sure.

He goes forth, knowing his life has changed, not knowing exactly how.

Sugar, Muhammad, and Me

One day in my seventh-grade social-studies class, in my usual "white-boy" voice, I answered a question correctly—it had to do with Sargent Shriver's relation to President Kennedy—and another boy's rough voice called from the back of the room, *"Who said that?"* I don't remember meeting this boy, though I recall how he introduced himself to me in the next few days: I walked into my math class and sat at my desk, then quickly hopped back up, two thumbtacks sticking out of my backside. At the end of class I asked a boy, whose name I've forgotten, if he knew who had put the tacks in my chair. "Everybody knows," he told me, and then he headed out to his next class.

This was the fall of 1975. I had graduated from Richardson Elementary the previous June and had now started at the local junior high, Kelly Miller. But another transition, in many ways more significant, had begun earlier. At some point between fifth and sixth grade, for the boys, The Change had taken place. They—we—had come to that stretch of the race in which our bodies were represented by the hare, our minds by the tortoise. The boys had always fought each other, but were now becoming capable of inflicting real harm; there had been talk of sex for several years, but our bodies were now urging some of us toward the real thing. Very little neutrality existed in any of this. There were fighters and there were those the fighters picked on; I was less than a hundred pounds of brown skin and ribs—maybe I don't need to say which group I was in. Gone was the deference, if not affection, that my smarts and proper speech had won me in elementary school. There, those attributes had made me student-council president. Here, they made me a target.

Then there was sex. There were the boys who had it; boys who talked a good game; boys, including me, who couldn't conceive of being in the first group and were too ignorant to join, or even know about, the second; and boys who were taunted mercilessly over their obvious virginity (pretty much the same as the third group).

This is run-of-the-mill stuff, which might otherwise live in my mind as an unpleasant but vague memory, an Expressionistic blur. Marvin Henderson, of the rough voice and thumbtacks, lends it clarity. I remember his high forehead; the relative lightness of his skin in our all-black school; his build, which was not highly defined but suggested strength; and his two front teeth, which jutted out at a forty-five-degree angle. I remember standing at my locker, where he'd come to torment me, and answering his casual, hard punches with shots that no doubt hurt my hand more than they hurt Marvin. I remember Marvin (not his real name) smiling and shaking his head, as if considering something both sad and funny, while telling his friends about me, "I'ma fuck him up." And I remember, vividly, the day he picked to do it.

By that fall the household at 232 had shrunk from its all-time high of seven to an all-time low of three: my mother, my grandmother, and me. Ma—who never did get a driver's license—got a ride to the Post Office each night from Uncle Nay or one of her co-workers. So from ten to seven the following morning, it was me and Grandma. I'm not sure it occurred to me to wonder who was looking out for whom. Ma may have shed some light on that: in the years to come, I heard her tell people that she didn't know what she would've done after my father's death if not for me, and I think she was alluding partly to Grandma. I am not, at least intellectually, a person who believes that everything happens for a reason; given the indiscriminate way that pain distributes itself, given the freakish way some people leave this life, I figure events occur because they can. Still, I sometimes catch myself having thoughts like: maybe *that's* why I was born, and why I came along half a generation after my siblings.

Wanda and Phyllis were off doing graduate work. Wayne, though, was still in the area. By then Wayne had begun his own career at the Post Office; he had filled out, and then some—he was a big man now; and he had taken a wife, Brenda. ("We were startin' to think he wasn't gonna *get* married," Uncle Manson said about my twenty-five-year-old brother.) He never said so, but I think Wayne saw it as his duty to pick up, if in kindlier fashion, where our father had left off in seeing that I developed manly interests. Wayne earned my eternal gratitude by taking me to sports events—many of them, and many kinds. Because of that, I'm sad for his sake that I didn't become a bigger sports fan. Today, for all the Washington Capitals hockey games we went to, I know the names of two hockey players, both surely retired by now, if not dead. Football to me is an assemblage of anonymous, oddly dressed men involved in an activity I comprehend only in its broadest outlines; might as well be opera. I'm a little better with baseball and basketball, but only a little. One sport stands as an exception—an ironic one—to all this, and my interest in it predates my outings with Wayne.

My awareness of boxing had started, several years earlier, with a mystery. It was early March of 1971, I was about to turn eight, and people in my neighborhood and on TV could talk of nothing but an upcoming fight between somebody named Muhammad Ali and another guy, Joe Frazier. The mystery had to do with still another fighter being mentioned—Cassius Clay. I pictured a scene like the climax of *The Good, the Bad and the Ugly*, with three men standing in a ring, eyeing one another warily, trying to decide whom to hit first.

Three and a half years later, with that confusion cleared up, I asked my father who he wanted to win the upcoming fight between Ali and the champ, the angry young giant George Foreman, and his answer (one of the last things he ever said to me, as it turned out) was, "Ali's got a big mouth, and I'd like to see Foreman shut it." Even then, that response seemed to me to miss the point about Ali. The Ali of the early 1970s had a big mouth, yes, but it wasn't one I wanted to see closed. That mouth let loose an affection for life as big as the world, a wonderful, humorous spirit almost too grand for one body to contain. He bragged with the best of them, yes, but that gleam in his eye let us know, if we would only see, that he didn't take it seriously. And like the best boxers, he carried his personality into his fights. In that battle against Foreman, which some feared Ali would not survive, let alone win (a legitimate concern, given Foreman's later admission that he always stepped into the ring with the hope of killing the man in there with him), Ali triumphed not only with his fists but with the sheer power of his *self*. Round after round, as Foreman slugged away, Ali lay against the ropes shielding himself with his arms and shouting "That all you got, George?," and it worked: poor Foreman answered every taunt with futile punches, wearing himself down until he was ready to be decked by Ali or, for that matter, by Ali's cleaning lady. Ali was a shining example of what a boxer is: a figure stepping into an adventure, certainly carrying with him the advice and wisdom of others, including younger versions of himself—but stepping in, in the end, alone, with only himself to rely on. In other words, an artist.

Of course, many of the fights Wayne and I saw did not involve artists; some of those guys were barely boxers. We went to a lot of matches at the very large, then-new Capital Centre, in Maryland, just over the DC line; even when our seats weren't very close to the ring, we could see on a gigantic screen what we might otherwise have missed, and when I think of it now, there seems to be a disconnect between the grandeur of the arena and equipment, on the one hand, and the pathetic nature of some of those poor under-card fighters on the other. A boxer in one heavyweight bout we saw wouldn't leave his corner, and laughter spread around the Cap Centre as people realized why: the seat of his trunks had split. Another heavyweight match took place between a comparatively fit boxer and another, very tall boxer with a stomach like a light-brown exercise ball. The first boxer landed punches on that stomach at will, and exclusively, maybe because it was the only part of his opponent he could reach; the owner of the stomach, for whom I felt bottomless pity, spent the match with a pained look on his face and his long arms outstretched, trying to smother the punches—as if a friendly argument between the two men had inexplicably gotten out of hand and he wanted to restore calm, as if he didn't know how he'd landed in this mess in the first place.

I thought I knew how he felt.

I never talked to Wayne about what was going on with Marvin Henderson. Usually there wasn't a chance to: often one of Wayne's co-workers, or his high-school friend Richard, went with us to the games or fights. But even when Wayne and I went by ourselves, driving to the Cap Centre at dusk, coming back in the dark, I never brought up Marvin. I knew more or less, and didn't need to hear, what Wayne would've said—something in line with what my mother had already told me: "If somebody hits you, I want you to try your best to kill him." As general advice that had its merits, but when it came to Marvin, my best seemed likely to leave the wrong person dead.

I didn't tell my friends about Marvin, either. I might have asked for help from Dana, the oldest of us and the best fighter, but I didn't. I can only guess now about why. Maybe I was afraid that Marvin might prove, to my horror, to be too much even for Dana; maybe I was afraid Dana would just tell me to fight my own battle; maybe I thought I would feel guilty if Dana fought my battle for me, successfully or not. My silence may have been the stoicism natural to boys that age, or it could have been my own severe strain of it. (Two decades after the events I am describing, I was approached about becoming a manager at the company where I worked then; when I asked why, the answer was, "Because you hold your cards about an inch from your vest.") Whatever the reason, I went about my life as if nothing was wrong. I did my homework, hung out with my friends, laughed at TV shows (*M*A*S*H* and *Barney Miller* and *Welcome Back, Kotter*), all while living in stomach-clenching dread of encounters with my tormentors, led by Marvin—about whom I spoke not one word.

Not all of the boxing matches Wayne and I attended were between bums. We saw some notable fighters, including, once, Wayne says, Larry Holmes in his pre-championship days. I don't remember that. Etched in my mind, though, are the times we saw Sugar Ray Leonard. Wayne took me to the Baltimore Civic Center to see Leonard, fresh from winning his Olympic gold medal, in his first professional fight: a six-rounder against one Luis "The Bull" Vega (who, Wayne later told me, was paid $600 as compared with Leonard's $30,000). By the end of the bout, Leonard had outpointed his carefully chosen opponent, but the thing I remember best happened early on. The Bull, perhaps trying to make things interesting, perhaps reasoning that he had nothing to lose, flew at Leonard like an escaped propeller, throwing lefts, rights, hooks, uppercuts, and one or two punches that had no names; while not one of those found its mark, the combination of them drove Leonard back against the ropes, where his face formed an expression that revealed everything there was to know about the cocky twenty-year-old—a bulging of the eyes and a drawing-together of the eyebrows that said, as clearly as if he'd spoken the words, *What's this guy doing? Doesn't he know I'm Sugar Ray Leonard?* Two years later, at the Cap Centre, Sugar took on Johnny Gant, who was a well-regarded fighter but not as famous as Leonard would become. Fans were divided in their predictions of who would win: Leonard, the youngster with energy and raw talent, or Gant, the older, seasoned pro. When the fight was over, fans were still divided—not against each other, but each within himself, and not over who had won, but over how they, the fans, felt about it. In the fight's final seconds, when Leonard's victory appeared just over the horizon, the crowd roared with excitement and anticipation; for a moment, as Gant was falling to the canvas, the arena became curiously still, breathless, quiet but for the echoes of the previous shouting; and when Gant was down, the place erupted anew—but this time the screams were tinged with sorrow, as if the eagerly awaited outcome, now that we had seen it, felt wrong somehow, like watching a young man knock down his father. And no one seemed to feel this more than Leonard, who grabbed a microphone and told the crowd, with condescension but obvious sincerity, "Let's hear it for Johnny Gant. He's a great fighter."

I was not a great fighter. I was not a good fighter, or a fighter of any kind. Far from looking on the showdown with Marvin as a chance to test myself, I would've avoided it altogether if that had been possible, which it did not seem to be. Because time moved more slowly in those days than it does now, I can't say for sure how long the Marvin business lasted. It may have been two weeks, or seven. I do remember hearing Marvin tell another boy one Monday that the next day, after our seventh-period social-studies class—the last class of the day—he was going to get me. "He'll prob'ly try to hook it," the other boy said. I didn't try to hook it. This was not bravery on my part; I simply knew that, to paraphrase Joe Louis, I could run but I couldn't hide.

That fall another showdown was shaping up, too: Ali's third match with Joe Frazier. That historic event took place in the Philippines, but Wayne and I caught it on the giant screen at the Cap Centre. Today I own a DVD of that fight, one of the most amazing things ever captured on film, and I appreciate, as I didn't at the time, what Ali faced. For fourteen rounds, Frazier, his body one large muscle, was relentlessness itself; he simply would not stop coming at Ali, and I honestly don't think anyone else could've stood up to his attack. Ali took advantage of his reach, dancing and hitting hard, making Frazier's face swell up, but he couldn't avoid the punishment, and in the late rounds he seemed on the edge of giving in to exhaustion—until a practically blind Frazier did so first. Smokin' Joe had come very, very close to winning, and he came even closer to granting my father's wish, achieving what George Foreman couldn't: shutting Ali's mouth. After the fight the only boasting the clearly spent Ali could manage was to call Frazier "the greatest fighter of all times, next to me." Ali looked stunned just to have gotten through the fight, which, he later said, was the closest he'd ever come to death.

The day Marvin chose to fuck me up, November 11, 1975, was—I would not dare put this in a work of fiction—a year to the day after my father died. (I have no love for November 11, and my first-born child gave me a scare when she nearly came into the world on that date.) That day stands unrivaled in my life for the fear I felt, and yet it was oddly peaceful; whether because of acceptance, or denial, or pure terror, or touches of all three, I moved around in a kind of trance. Perhaps because of that state, perhaps because I am gazing back through the fog of nearly four decades, I have the impression that when other boys looked at and spoke to me that day, there was something in their faces and voices that was like sympathy.

I didn't learn much in that day's social-studies class. After it was over I left the room to find Marvin standing just outside the door, hands at his sides. The whole class stood behind him, quiet as churchgoers, watching, waiting. I walked up to Marvin; there was nowhere else to go.

Marvin said, "You ready?"

"No."

He hit me—slapped me, really—on my cheek. The class, with one voice, went, "Ooooooo." I put my hand to my face. He hit me again.

And then something inside me snapped. I didn't think about how much bigger and stronger Marvin was; all I knew at that moment was that he had made my life hell for no good reason, and my fear was replaced by rage.

Before I realized what I was doing, I charged him; the next thing I knew, I was on the floor with Marvin, trying to get in a good punch. Soon we were on our feet again, facing each other. It was my bad luck at that point to have a wall behind me. Marvin pushed me, hard. My head hit the wall. I sensed dimly that I was sliding down the wall to the floor, and I discovered something interesting: people really do see stars, just like in cartoons, when they're knocked unconscious.

I later heard Marvin say what he had planned to do to me while I was on the floor, and it's possible I would have died that day had my social-studies teacher not come out of the room when she did. Pulled to my feet, semi-conscious, I was aware of my teacher standing between Marvin and me, saying something to both of us, like the referee in a boxing match that had taken place in reverse. Then the crowd broke up, and Marvin left with them. I went home with a lump on my head. The Marvin episode was over.

This story has a couple of postscripts. One day two years later, during ninth grade, I sat in art class near two boys whose given names I've forgotten. One of them was nicknamed Eggy, for the shape of his head. Something reminded Eggy of my fight with Marvin, which he had witnessed, and he described it to the other boy.

Other Boy: "Who won?"

Eggy: "Marvin—"

Other Boy: "That's what I thought."

Eggy: "—He banged Clifford's head decent."

Other Boy: "Did Clifford cry?"

Eggy: "Nah, that nigger ain't get up off a tear."

I count that last line among my life's trophies.

On an afternoon in the summer of 1982, on a street in northwest Washington, I ran into Jerry Banks, who had attended junior high school with me. Jerry told me, among other things, that in the years since then he had once seen Marvin leaving a party, high on the drug of the moment and waving a pistol in the air. He also told me that Marvin was serving twenty to forty-five years in prison for homicide.

So, given that I had to meet Marvin Henderson at all, I had done it at a good time. And even walking home after the fight with him, I felt an odd kind of luck. Unlike Ali, I had not triumphed. But like him, I had a sense of wonder over simply having survived.

Interlude

The principal at Kelly Miller Junior High was Claude E. Moten, a fairly large, coal-black man who wore three-piece suits, glasses, and a short Afro; he had a deep, resonant voice and what could be called, at the risk of understatement, a no-nonsense attitude. (In his office Mr. Moten kept a wooden paddle, with holes drilled in it, that I once saw him apply to the backside of one of my fellow students. I realized later that the holes were there so that air would not slow the paddle's journey toward its target.) Mr. Moten made attempts at inspiration as well as discipline—one attempt, anyway. When I was in eighth grade he announced that the school's theme song for the year—a new concept—would be a 1975 hit by Harold Melvin and the Blue Notes, "Wake Up Everybody." ("Wake up, everybody, no more sleeping in bed / No more backward thinking, time for thinking ahead . . .") What that mainly meant was that at assemblies, Mr. Moten would say, "And what's our theme for this year?" To which we students, who knew what was good for us, would answer, "Wake up, EVERYBODY!" (The next year the song was "The Greatest Love of All," a hit for George Benson in 1977, but Mr. Moten was so attached to his original choice that he couldn't mention Benson's song without saying something about Melvin's, too.)

Two things have long interested me about pop songs. One is that their music can often make the stupidest lyrics sound good. (The late Steve Allen built a whole comedy routine on the inverse observation.) Even the lyrics to "Wake Up Everybody," which are thoughtful for those of a mainstream hit, suffer a bit without the melody. "The world has changed so very much from what it used to be," the singer tells us; "There is so much hatred, war and poverty . . ." Anyone who thought there was more hatred, war, and poverty in 1975 than in 1945, 1935, or 1915 would have been well advised to pick up a history book, but no matter; today I still feel happy when I hear the song. Which brings me to the other thing I find interesting about pop songs (maybe I'm alone in this, but maybe not): I enjoy catching snatches of the ones from my youth, in supermarkets, in department stores, or on car radios, no matter what was happening in those long-ago days when I first heard them. My junior-high years, to make another understatement, were not the happiest of my life; so why doesn't Maxine Nightingale's 1976 song "Right Back Where We Started From" make me want to get right back where I was before I heard it? Why, instead, does it trigger in me a brief but intense, not unpleasurable yearning for something I can't quite name? Does it have to do with some inherent, wistful, haunting quality in the song itself ("Do you remember that day—that sunny day—when you first came my way . . .")? Or is the association not as bad as I think: did I, in spite of the misery of that era, sense that things would get better one day soon, that I had most of my life in front of me?

Comics, Music, Movies, Novels, and the Limits of Alienation

Sometimes life, like a movie theater, shows you previews—mysterious, exciting glimpses of paths you can follow if you choose. The real-life versions don't announce themselves; you are denied the joy of anticipating them, and their sweetness is pure for only an instant, trailing away afterward like blood in water, mingling with the memory of what they portended.

The preview I got in the summer of 1975—one of them—really was like the kind in a theater, because it involved pictures. At Landover Mall in Maryland, just over the DC line, I stood in a bookstore thumbing through a large paperback called *Origins of Marvel Comics*. This book had straight text but also artwork, what looked to be reproductions of comic-book stories; because the art was printed not on the color-muting newsprint of regular comic books but on gleaming white paper, the reds, yellows, and blues exploded from the pages. Here were the Hulk, the Submariner, Spider-Man, and Thor, the heroes of the comics for which I had long trekked to the bottom of Division Avenue, illustrated more excitingly, and in some cases more primitively, than I'd ever seen them; imagine happening upon a gathering of everyone you ever liked or admired, a party where the only person missing was you.

I put *Origins* back on the shelf and left the mall with whoever had brought me. But the book stayed on my mind, and the next time we went to the mall, I asked someone to please buy it for me. (Phyllis laughed when I pronounced "origins" with the stress on the second syllable; I thought it was supposed to sound like "original.") I got my wish, and at twelve I went home with one of the half-dozen most important books of my life.

Origins of Marvel Comics, by Stan Lee, detailed the way my favorite superheroes had come into being in the early 1960s ('round about the same time I did). Stan "The Man" did no drawing, but he conceived of the Marvel heroes and scripted their early adventures. In *Origins* he devoted a section each to five Marvel titles: *The Fantastic Four, The Incredible Hulk, The Amazing Spider-Man, The Mighty Thor*, and (my least favorite) *Dr. Strange*. Each section began with a five- or six-page chapter of Lee's prose, explaining how he had come up with the character (or group, in the case of The Fantastic Four), followed by a reprint of the series' first issue, then by a reprint of a later issue, to show how the series had developed. Lee (who is still alive as I write this) knows his way around the English language, and his prose in *Origins*, like his narrative sections of the Marvel comic books, is wonderful—not only grammatically sound but full of wit and humor. More important to me at the time, though, was that *Origins* shed light on the Marvel characters themselves. The book provided starting points for tracing the heroes' story lines, clearing up all my lingering confusion from having jumped into the series in the middle. And most illuminating of all, Lee spelled out what I had dimly perceived in my previous forays into the world of Marvel: the real differences between Marvel characters and other superheroes. The DC heroes were perfectly, if unbelievably, well-adjusted; Batman's alter-ego, Bruce Wayne, as he was portrayed in those days, was a millionaire man-about-town and so had not one but two fulfilling lives. The same seemed to be true of Superman's alter-ego, Clark Kent, although why Kent felt fulfilled is hard to imagine, since the only woman he ever came near was his fellow reporter Lois Lane, who dismissed Kent as a milquetoast while she pined for Superman. But Lee maintained—and in those days I believed—that Marvel heroes were what real, lusty, flawed human beings would be like if they happened to have super powers. The Thing paid a price for his power: the "cosmic rays" that gave him great strength also made him ugly as homemade sin, and he had trouble being philosophical about it. Peter Parker, the brainy, friendless nerd of a teenager who unbeknownst to the rest of the world was really Spider-Man, was a younger Clark Kent—complete with the grinding frustration a real Kent would experience. Spider-Man fought all manner of super-powered lunatics, protecting a public that nonetheless considered him a villain—and so was an outcast in not only one but two worlds. Here was a guy who had it worse than *I* did.

To my twelve-year-old mind, this was profundity. After I read *Origins*, I was pretty much done with Superman and Batman; Marvel was the company for me.

When Phyllis came home from Princeton during the Christmas holidays of 1975, she and I went exploring for places that sold comic books; she cared nothing for them, but she knew what they meant to me. Our mission led us, via two buses, across the city to Georgetown, where we found the place that corresponded to my idea of heaven: the Key Bridge News Stand, a hole in the wall that housed more new and vintage comics than I had known existed in one place. Here they were, contained by the hundred in box after box, each in its own plastic sleeve: back issues of *Spider-Man* drawn by Steve Ditko, *The Hulk* drawn by Herb Trimpe, *Thor* drawn by the king himself, Jack Kirby—all written by Stan the Man. At the end of our first visit to Key Bridge, Phyllis plunked down $8.40 for the books I wanted—an amount still fixed in my brain, for some reason, and one that seemed, to everybody else around me, an insane sum to spend on comics. I couldn't have stopped smiling if I'd tried, and Phyllis, nearly as happy as I was, took me on more trips to the shop over the next couple of years.

Thor appealed to me for much the same reason that *The Godfather* did: I loved the majesty, wealth of ceremonial detail, and complex familial relationships of those two tales of dynasty. Lee had Thor, the Norse god of thunder, speak in a kind of latter-day Shakespearean English that, for me, added to the sense of grandeur. (My friends were less favorably impressed. "I hate the way he talk," Big Darryl said. Little Darryl once asked, "He gotta say all that before he can fight?") Kirby was the right artist to illustrate Thor, since he drew *everybody* to look like a god; as illustrated by Kirby, for example, Reed Richards of The Fantastic Four—when he wasn't stretched out like human taffy—had the same square jaws as Thor and was just about as muscular. For that reason, as Lee pointed out in *Origins*, Ditko was a better choice to bring the wiry Spider-Man to life; Ditko's drawings had an odd, spare elegance, a simplicity that could give certain boys the mistaken idea that they could draw just as well. (Ditko was Lester Young, he of the deceptively spare tenor-sax lines, to Kirby's Coleman Hawkins, who blew with enough force to take out your windowpanes.) Herb Trimpe drew the Hulk not as a perfectly proportioned god but as a monstrous green mass of muscle. Following the Hulk was, in a way, like following Muhammad Ali: the toughest guy on the planet, he nonetheless had enemies who were quite adept at letting him know he'd been in a fight. Where Ali had Joe Frazier, George Foreman, and Ken Norton, the Hulk had the Rhino, the Abomination, and Doc Samson.

While reading the adventures of the Marvel heroes, I continued to create my own comics. Vulcan, the Roman god of fire—black, as drawn by me—was a direct response to Thor; the teenage Spider-Man inspired, to some extent, my high-school heroes Doc Gravity and Prince Power. (I'm not sure who influenced Microman the Unsung Hero—Ant-Man, maybe?) At the same time, my methods got a little more sophisticated. Moving on from 8 ½-by-11-inch typing paper, I began drawing on larger, thicker sheets of Bristol board, and I gave up ball-point pens for felt-tip markers and fountain pens with different-sized, removable nibs. Instead of using, for example, the edge of the weekly *Washington Post TV Week* to draw straight lines, I got a long metal ruler worthy of an architect, carefully measuring panels; rather than making stories up as I drew them, which had been my approach in the days of the Canary, I wrote scripts in pencil on loose-leaf paper, complete with descriptions of each panel's contents. (Whereas at Marvel the scripting, drawing, inking, and lettering were each done by a different person, I was a one-man band.) I noticed that my own face would take on whatever expression I was laboring to draw on the face of a character.

The crowning touch came on Christmas Day 1977, during my ninth-grade year, when my family gave me a drafting table. If I had to name the single greatest gift I ever received, that might have to be it. As drafting tables go, my wooden model was a little thing, but *God*, how thrilled I was to get it. It was placed against the edge of the partial wall separating the living and dining rooms, and for the remainder of my years at 232 I was often placed there as well, hunched over and happy. As for my drawing, it still left one or two things to be desired. But: it was getting better.

===

One day, for reasons I don't remember now, and using a word he alone among my friends would have chosen, Big Darryl observed about me that I had four "passions": riding my skateboard, collecting comic books, drawing comics of my own, and buying records.

The records I bought, initially 45 rpm singles with B sides, were the soul/R&B/funk radio hits of the day: "Do It (Til You're Satisfied)" by BT Express, "Skin Tight" by the Ohio Players, "Hollywood Swingin'" by Kool & the Gang, "Tell Me Something Good" by Rufus and Chaka Khan. In the summer of '75 I graduated to LPs, with *That's the Way of the World* by Earth, Wind & Fire, which I played every single day.

But that summer, which was the same season that I discovered *Origins of Marvel Comics*, part of me set off on a parallel musical track, which in retrospect was not unconnected to the Marvel influence. It started when I went with my sisters and a cousin to see *Cooley High*. The movie is set in 1964 in a black community in Chicago, much like the one where I grew up in Washington. It tells the story of two high-school boys: Cochise, a handsome, smart, popular basketball star, and his best friend, Preach, who wears glasses, reads and writes poetry, and studies history books "for fun"—but who, because he spends so much time cutting up with Cochise, has "the worst grades in three states," as one of his teachers puts it. What made *Cooley High* so appealing for me, in part, was what the Cochise-Preach friendship represented: a meeting of the nerdy boy I was with the popular boy I dreamt of being. (I hadn't worked out for myself how I might become popular while spending most of my free time at home drawing.) The fantasy was so beguiling because it had a foothold in reality. Preach was what the average person of some intelligence and creativity (myself, say) might see if he looked in the mirror; Cochise was what that same person would see in his daydreams. Two halves of the same guy. There was Preach, having his notebook snatched away by two of his pals, who read his verse aloud in front of him, between howls of laughter; but then there was Cochise, consoling Preach privately by saying, "What they know?"—Cochise, who was the first chosen for the basketball team in gym class, who won a college scholarship, who got the girls (which Preach finally did, too: fantasy temporarily made real). The movie's basis in the actual is confirmed in the climax, when the fantasy of Cochise comes to an irrevocable end, and reality—in the form of Preach—is left behind, grieving and guilt-stricken.

Parts of *Cooley High* were just real enough to make me believe in, and want, the fantasy. I didn't dream of being Preach because, in a couple of important ways, I already was Preach. I wanted to be Cochise, which was why I asked my mother for a Washington Redskins jacket, the kind with leather sleeves and a velvet torso: it was the closest thing I knew of to the jacket Cochise wore.

But what really got me about the movie was the music. *Cooley High*, set in the 1960s, had a soundtrack made up of songs from that era. Preach's romance unfolded to the sound of the Temptations' "My Girl," and once I discovered that that was yet another record my siblings had left behind in the basement, it became my personal theme music; I must have driven my mother crazy spinning that song on my dinky little record player. "My Girl" opened my mind to the idea of music that you *didn't* hear every day on the radio, music that set my tastes apart from others'.

That was important, because, while part of me fantasized about being as popular as Cochise, another part embraced how separate I felt from other kids. My indifference to Preach notwithstanding, I was attracted to characters who reflected some of the separateness I felt. In eighth grade I read J. D. Salinger's *The Catcher in the Rye* for school, and while I hesitate to add to the trillion words already written about Holden Caulfield, he made alienation seem cooler than Charlie Brown ever had. (My problem with Preach may have been that he wasn't alienated *enough*.) And it makes perfect sense that one of my favorite Marvel Comics characters—rivaled in his alienation only by Spider-Man—was the Silver Surfer, a gleaming, highly powerful but peace-loving alien trapped on Earth, whose skies he mournfully traveled on his surfboard as he lamented the savagery of humankind. Like the Silver Surfer, I felt that fate had cruelly placed me among people—my junior-high classmates—who were as weird to me as I was to them. In my mind I *was* the Silver Surfer. (And I rode my skateboard so skillfully that I could coast down Division Avenue while reading my latest Marvel purchase.) The big difference between us was that the Silver Surfer could fight like nobody's business—though he had to be provoked. (Little Darryl's take on the Silver Surfer: "He don't like to fight. That's the only thing I don't like about him.")

Anyway, "My Girl" sent me to the basement to see what else Wayne, Wanda, and Phyllis had left behind. ("Them records prehistoric," Big Darryl once said, to the delight of Little Darryl.) I found an album by David Ruffin, a singer in the Motown mold; the album included "What Becomes of the Brokenhearted." The song opens with what sounds like a bass drum, pounded slowly, followed by a chorus of wordless vocals delivered in reverent tones; the pomp, the solemnity of those sounds were worthy of Thor. Enter Ruffin, singing the lines, "As I walk this land of broken dreams / I have visions of many things . . ." Oh, man, there it was: the lines evoked a lone figure, a self-described dreamer, on a journey over a landscape where things were not what they should have been, lamenting what he saw—this was me, the Silver Surfer, brilliant but oh so misunderstood. For all that, "What Becomes of the Brokenhearted" turned out to be just another song about needing love but not finding it, but as a boy of thirteen/fourteen who liked girls but didn't know the first thing about approaching them, I could relate to that, too. I played the song even more relentlessly than I'd played "My Girl."

I was friendly with a tall, pudgy, pretty smart boy named John Banks, who managed—as who did not?—to be more acceptable among our peers than a non-fighting, non-fucking, white-talking brainiac sissy punk like me. One day John said to me, "You swear you troubled!" He could not have put it more accurately. As I drifted away from Dana and the Darryls and the rest of the Simple City crowd and dragged myself through my days at Kelly Miller, getting nearly straight A's, avoiding punches when I could, hitting back with my bony arms when I couldn't, drawing when my homework was finished, playing those old songs, laughing at Wayne's old Bill Cosby records, washing dishes, fixing my mother very simple meals when she got up for the night shift, staying up late for Johnny Carson long after my grandmother was asleep, I nurtured my misery like a kind of plant, glorying in my aloneness, the proof that I was, well, special. I was, of course, setting myself up for a fall. More than one, as it happened.

===

The way I learned how music actually works came about because of my friendship with a boy named Ronald. We met in eighth grade, our second year of junior high, and quickly discovered that we'd had very similar bad experiences in seventh grade. We began walking from class to class together and talking on the phone in the evenings. "It's kind of cool," he told me, "to meet somebody who's been through the wringer as bad as I have, if not worse." Ronald was smart, maybe smarter than me, but he was also unfocused and a tad lazy, so his grades weren't as good. And he was—well, his nickname was "Crazy Ronald," for the partly genuine, partly affected nutty streak that was his defense mechanism. I thought he was hilarious. He did things, little things, that no one else—no one else at Kelly Miller, anyway—would have thought of. Once I got a glimpse of a class assignment he turned in; as we were required to do, he had written his name in an upper corner, followed by his homeroom number, after which he had put in parentheses, "Not that it matters." If I sounded like a white boy, Ronald sounded like a white boy who had spent the morning sniffing airplane glue; he said many things in a weird voice, which I began to imitate, just as I did that side-to-side walk of his, so completely had I come under his spell. One day, when I telephoned the girl who was the object of my first all-out crush and tried to make her remember who I was, she said, "You're the one who tries to act like that other boy."

Ronald played piano and was friends with a handful of other musical types. I felt a little left out of their special brand of camaraderie, and for that reason as much as any other, the summer after eighth grade—1977—I enrolled in the DC Youth Orchestra Program. I took up the clarinet, which is how I learned about notes, scales, time signatures, and all the rest. For someone to whom music is so important, I turned out not to be particularly good at playing it; I had a certain ability, but it had definite limits, which I reached with impressive speed. I blew—literally—through the beginning, advanced-beginning, and preparatory classes, leaving behind some kids who had started before me; I had a lot of fun in elementary band, did pretty well in elementary orchestra, got by in junior band, and finally, somehow, got into junior orchestra, the level just below the actual Youth Orchestra, where I proceeded to illustrate what is called the Peter Principle—coming to a stop at my "level of incompetence," or, in this case, colliding with it like a crash-test dummy with a stone wall. One of the most humiliating experiences I had during those years—actually, in my life—came one day during rehearsal, when, for some reason, I was the only clarinet player present. The conductor was a young black woman who could've moonlighted as a model; puzzled by something she heard, or didn't hear, while the whole ensemble was playing, she quieted the other kids and had me play my part unaccompanied, walking to where I sat in order to hear better. She might as well have asked me to flap my arms and fly to the moon. It became very clear, very soon, that I couldn't play the part I was supposed to have practiced, and I expected to get a tongue-lashing like I'd never known. What the conductor did instead was both better and worse: standing behind me as I huffed, puffed, and butchered the clarinet lines, she draped her arm gently, lovingly, on my shoulders, a gesture that meant, *You poor boy.*

Ironically, not long after I had signed up for the Youth Orchestra Program, my friendship with Ronald—which was principally what had led me to join—began to deteriorate. Maybe he was jealous of my standing with the teachers at Kelly Miller while I was jealous of his friendships with other musical kids. Whatever the cause, by the start of ninth grade Ronald and I, inseparable the previous year, had begun to approach each other like two alley cats. Once, we were both crossing a room, on collision course; seeing each other, we stopped simultaneously and made the same wordless, sarcastic gesture at the same time: a sweeping hand motion that meant, *Far be it from me to interrupt your obviously important journey.* On my side, at least, that kind of behavior was meant to cover up bewilderment: *What have I done to make you hate me? How did we get to this point?* In the middle of that fall, Ronald transferred to the Duke Ellington School for the Arts, and that was that.

I was, at fourteen-going-on-fifteen, all but friendless. I hung out some with John Banks ("You swear you troubled!"), who for all his teasing ways liked me, but I kept him at arm's length, feeling that he didn't understand me. (The real problem may have been that he understood me too well.) I tried to lose myself in comics, old music, and the rest of my nerdy pursuits, but there was no getting around the six-plus hours a day eaten up by that maximum-security prison everyone else insisted on calling school, and the pleasure I got from contemplating my own alienation had come to its end. I missed Ronald, and I couldn't use John as a port in the storm because he attended a different junior high. I wasn't as miserable as I'd been in the Marvin Henderson days, but that was about it for the bright side.

One morning in the spring of 1978, my great stoicism cracked. I was so upset about the prospect of another day at school that Ma told me I didn't have to go—I tagged along while she did errands downtown instead. Ma now understood, if she hadn't before, how unhappy I was.

Many years later, at our mother's funeral, Phyllis used a French phrase to describe her: *il faut cultiver notre jardin*, which translates as "we must cultivate our garden." Ma, she said, was a simple woman with no pretenses to an intellectual life; rather, she took good care of the things and people in her small domain. Ma was also a generous woman with a good sense of humor—though you couldn't tell that from photographs, for which her expression invariably changed to stone. And once in a while, up to the end of her life, she could surprise me. A small example: one day many years after I had finished high school, I was clowning around with my mother and said to her nonsensically, "But Ma, I don't *want* to go to the prom!" Without missing a beat, she said, "Go on and skip it then. Don't let tradition stop you from being who you are."

My mother (she was around five-three or five-four and not big around; get thoughts of Hattie McDaniel out of your head)—my little mother knew what she was about in her life. *Cultivating her garden*: When she saw how I felt about public school, she knew what she had to do, and the two of us began looking for alternatives for tenth grade and beyond. That was how we found St. Anthony's, a small, private Catholic school in Northeast Washington, near Catholic University, a Metro-ride away from my house. There were other parochial schools in the city, but St. Anthony's was the only one that was co-ed. "I want you to be around some girls," Ma said, and I didn't argue. The tuition was close to $1,000 per year, which was not a trifling sum for a postal clerk in 1978. But she did it for her baby boy.

===

The now-defunct St. Anthony's High had a total of about two hundred fifty students, nearly all of them black. The summer before I started there, I was a little worried: would this private school be the first place where I wouldn't stand out academically, where I would struggle to keep up? It took me about a week to establish myself once more as Smart Boy, owing partly, again, to the sound of the correct answers I gave in class—this time not so much their diction as their depth, the new rumble of a baritone/bass issuing from a hundred-and-twenty-pound body. The other difference this time was that nobody wanted to beat me up. I was still a nerd, but in my seventy-person class I was an acceptable, even likable, nerd. For the first time in three years,

I didn't have knots in my stomach every morning at the thought of going to school.

On my first day at St. Anthony's, walking through the front door, I saw a lanky guy in a white shirt and tie sitting on the three steps of the small lobby. This was Kevin Harris, whom I'd last seen in the '72 session of the Summer Program, when he and his partner in the talent show, three guys short, were the Jackson 2. (Halfway through the song he was singing, Kevin forgot the words, prompting shouts from the audience: "*Dance*, Kevin!") Now, in 1978, Kevin and I recognized each other instantly, and pretty much from that day, we were inseparable for the next three years.

Kevin was a friendly, good-hearted guy who was even shyer around girls and even skinnier (though several inches taller) than I was. And we had something else in common: among the things he'd been up to in the six years since I'd last seen him was making his own comics. He had drawn, off and on, a newspaper-style strip called "Fang & Midnight," after his cat (Midnight) and dog (Fang). If I had come under Ronald's spell, Kevin came under mine, and my comics inspired him to draw more "Fang & Midnight" strips. We became known among our St. A's classmates as the cartoonists, helped by the way we signed our homework and other assignments (Kev was "The Great Cartoonist," I was "Cartoonist Extraordinaire").

My own comics had improved. The stories, at least in the context of the superhero genre, had begun to make actual sense, and the drawings had gotten to be pretty good. My teachers and classmates thought they looked professional—at least they said so. And whereas in the past, the labor-intensiveness of the drawing, inking, and coloring sometimes led me to abandon a superhero before I had finished even one story, just before the start of high school I settled on the character who would carry me through many episodes to the peak of my (completely unheralded) performance as a creator of comics. Nineteen-seventy-eight saw the birth of the Telstar. Named for the communications satellite, the Telstar had powers that corresponded to it: he could fly, and he was able to send telepathic messages. Best—or worst—of all, he had a special weapon, the telepunch, meaning that he could throw a haymaker whose impact was absorbed by the jaw of a villain across the room. Plus he had great strength, for some reason. The Telstar wore blue leggings and gloves, a gray hooded sweatshirt with a black

"T" over the heart, and specially made goggles that allowed him to see each otherwise invisible telepunch as it sped through the air. Underneath the suit he was Gene Brady, a black student at Lawrenceville Prep (a school I knew about because of Phyllis—it was near Princeton). The story of the Telstar's origin was straight out of Marvel. Frustrated over the state of his love life, the egghead Gene went off to lose himself by experimenting in the school's science lab late at night. Something went wrong, and the resulting explosion gave Gene his special powers. Like Marvel characters, Gene knew frustration; in retrospect, though, Gene's troubles were related less to super-power-induced angst than to the usual problems of a normal, if shy and awkward, teenager—which I just happened to be when I was drawing him. Also like the Marvel heroes, and like Ali, the Telstar had a roster of enemies he fought regularly: the Matador, who took on bulls and the Telstar with his bare fists; the Bird of Prey, whose golden-brown suit and cape—complete with a hood that kept his face in shadow—allowed him to fly and menace the public; Westar, the (literal) strongman leader of a rogue nation, whom the CIA blackmailed the Telstar into fighting by threatening to reveal his (the Telstar's) secret identity; and the Victim, who as a result of radiation from nuclear testing had strength to rival the Telstar's as well as the power to aim small-scale explosions. (The Victim's costume was black except for a lavender circle over the left side of his chest; I nearly named him the Purple Heart.)

I want very much to write here that I made copies of the Telstar stories, distributed them to local newsstands and Georgetown coffeehouses, and watched as my comics became a local underground hit. Even if that had happened, you probably still wouldn't have heard of the Telstar before now—so why don't we pretend it's true?

I led Kevin on some comics-related expeditions. Because I had gotten it into my head that the first stop on the road to fame was to get our stuff copyrighted, we followed a circuitous route that started at the Library of Congress and ended at an office in a Virginia suburb, where a thirty-ish, mustached white guy granted Kevin and me our copyrights—smiling and shaking his head the whole time, no doubt amused to be dealing with two black boys who looked younger than their sixteen years. More world-weary was the middle-aged, heavyset man in the office in downtown DC whom we approached about selling the Telstar and Fang & Midnight to a national syndicate. At the man's suggestion I tried turning the Telstar into a black-and-white, daily-newspaper-style strip. The man looked at those, then asked to see more; he never told me I was wasting my time, but neither did he offer to pitch my stuff to a syndicate, and eventually I gave up in frustration. Kev didn't make it too far, either.

The experience didn't dampen the fun of writing and drawing the Telstar stories. In fact, I enjoyed myself even more than before, because life at 232 had gotten less lonely. My sisters had come home! Phyllis, with a master's degree in religious ethics from Princeton under her belt, returned and taught at Georgetown University—where dismay over her salary, among other things, soon led her a couple of miles away, to George Washington University Law School. Wanda, who now had a PhD, used 232 as a base while she started out in the field of psychology. Then as now, I had to be alone when I wrote, but while I was drawing at my drafting table, I liked the company of my sisters. Sometimes we were all quiet together, working; sometimes we chatted while the TV was on. (It was Wanda who could come the closest of any of us to cutting through the old Thompson politesse. Once, when Wayne told me he was taking me somewhere and then forgot, and I was giving the family line—"Oh, well"—Wanda said to me, "Stop being such a good *sport* all the time!")

The summer of 1980, between my junior and senior years of high school, was my first in four years not spent with the Youth Orchestra Program. While Uncle Brock and Aunt Catherine were squabbling up the street; while Uncle Nay worked outside and Aunt Emma cooked and cleaned inside; while Uncle Manson and Aunt Lucy did I'm-not-sure-what; while Wayne and Brenda adopted a son, Eric, and Wayne approached his first anniversary as an ordained Baptist minister; while Ma and Wanda went back and forth to work; while Phyllis had a summer-associate gig at the law firm where she would later be a partner; and while Grandma rose at five a.m. to make sugar-loaded coffee and butter-soaked toast, watched soaps in the afternoon, and then looked out the window or sat on the porch glider the rest of the day, I drew comics and did not much else. Kev didn't do anything that summer, either. Sometimes we sat in my basement or his and talked about girls; other times, we entertained each other in silly ways, making up, for example, an all-black cast for *M*A*S*H* (Hawkeye Pierce became Black

Eyed Peas, Hot Lips was Fat Lips, Frank Burns was Burnt Franks, etc.). And sometimes, our combined nothingness left us even more bored than we were separately. Once, I recall, I wanted to go to Georgetown to check out a chess shop. (Just to complete my nerd profile, I had started a chess club at St. Anthony's during my junior year.) Since we did so much else together, I felt obligated to ask Kev if he wanted to go with me; having been asked, he felt obligated to say yes. And so there we were, making our cranky way across town, he not wanting to go and I not particularly wanting him with me. Sometimes we couldn't even manage activities as pathetic as that. A phone call one morning went like this:

Me: "Hey, what're you doing?"

Kev: "Nothing. Ain't nothing to *do.*"

On the other hand, I drew some good comics that summer. During that stretch, as I recall, the Telstar won a thrilling come-from-behind victory in a slugfest with the Victim. Meanwhile, other things were brewing in my brain, even if I didn't know it.

On a Saturday night at the tail end of the previous school year—I'm almost sure it was the night of my junior prom, which I didn't attend—I watched *The Graduate* on television. I was mesmerized. Here, in the immediacy of film, was a third incarnation of the figure who had struck a chord with me in other mediums: the romantic outsider, seen first in the guise of Charlie Brown in comics and then Holden Caulfield in literature. Dustin Hoffman's Benjamin Braddock in *The Graduate* was that outsider as quasi–action hero, a Marvel Comics misfit without costume or special powers—jumping in his sports car at the climax to go after his beloved Elaine, running out of gas and then taking off on foot, getting to Elaine's wedding too late but, hold on, maybe not too late after all. The movie crystallized what I had loved about Charlie Brown and Holden, made me able to articulate my attraction to the idea of the young-man-not-quite-fitting-in; it also made me want, as I realized on some level, to take a crack at portraying that young man myself. (Plus, *The Graduate* expanded my musical horizons: I became a fan of Simon & Garfunkel—not exactly the rage in northeast DC; neither were the Beatles, whom I had also started listening to.)

Then came a weekday in August of 1980, a long, hot, empty summer day of the kind that doesn't seem to exist anymore. Wandering alone in northwest, I randomly and casually went into Brentano's, a bookstore on F Street at the time. Despite my reputation as an egghead, despite my fascination with my third-grade Afro-American history book, despite how much I loved the writing in Stan Lee's comics, I could probably have counted on the fingers of one hand the non-illustrated books I had read in my seventeen years. There were maybe five Hardy Boys books; there was *The Autobiography of Buffalo Bill,* which I had chosen, for some reason, as the subject of a seventh-grade book report; there was *The Autobiography of Malcolm X,* which that boy had sneered at me for reading, and which I hadn't even finished and wouldn't until I was nearly thirty; there was James Fennimore Cooper's novel *The Deerslayer,* the topic of a book report in eleventh grade; and there was *The Catcher in the Rye.* If there was more, I don't remember. And so, as I browsed the shelves in Brentano's, picking up a book here and there, I had very little to guide me, beyond titles and covers. Somehow, in my near-total ignorance, I made it to *The Sun Also Rises.*

I'll never forget standing there and reading the novel's first sentence. Before that, the few novels I'd picked up began in ways that made it clear I was reading literature with a big "L," works communicating thought from on high. *The Deerslayer'*s first sentence was, "On the human imagination, events produce the effects of time." Even Holden Caulfield took a step back, or up, to begin his story: "If you really want to hear about it . . . "

But here was the first line of this guy Hemingway's *The Sun Also Rises*: "Robert Cohn was once middleweight boxing champion of Princeton." That was it. The sentence's simplicity, specificity, and matter-of-factness hit me like a sucker punch. I read more. For some reason I left the book in the store, but when I got home I discovered someone's copy of the very same edition—minus the front cover—in the good old basement of 232.

So began my reading life. For the rest of that summer, and into the fall, I read other books left by my siblings in the basement, books of the kind taught in every American high school except, it seemed, mine: Hemingway's *Old Man and the Sea*, Salinger's *Franny and Zooey*, Orwell's *1984* and *Animal Farm*, Steinbeck's *Of Mice and Men*, Vonnegut's *Slaughterhouse-Five*, and John Knowles's somewhat Catcher-like *A Separate Peace*, which I particularly enjoyed. Returning to the bookstore, I picked up Tom Robbins's novel *Still Life with Woodpecker*, based mostly on its cover, which vaguely but purposely resembled a pack of Camel cigarettes (Ma's brand); that book led me to others of Robbins's works—freaky, mind-blowing stuff for a virgin who had never been drunk or high. I bought a copy of William Goldman's novel *Marathon Man*, which among other things hipped me to the existence of egg creams. I even tried making some for Kev and me, not realizing they didn't actually call for the raw eggs I put in. It's a lucky thing I didn't kill us both.

The previous school year, as a junior, I had taken the PSAT. In themselves my scores were nothing to jump up and down about, but because I was black they got me some attention from colleges. The very first piece of mail I got came from someplace called Oberlin, in Ohio. As senior year ground on, and I began looking at colleges more seriously, I noticed that Oberlin had a creative-writing program.

Meanwhile, even as I began to set aside comic books in favor of novels, I kept drawing. I even started to develop a defensive attitude about it. These were the days before Art Spiegelman's *Maus*, which gave comic books a measure of respectability even in the eyes of many people who didn't normally read them; in the early '80s, the prevailing view was that they were created by people of little sophistication for those of even less. I was eager to refute that idea—so eager, in fact, that the essay accompanying my application to Oberlin was a defense of comics. (A couple of people, on hearing this, seemed to question my sanity. But hey, I got in.)

In retrospect, my stance seems to me the protectiveness people feel toward things they're in danger of losing. Since I'd started the Telstar series, my drawing had improved dramatically, sometimes within the same story; by now, though, the improvement had tapered off. I was at the top of my game. It was like throwing a rock with all my might—at the moon: for one brief, glorious instant in its arc, it hung there, framed in light, my best; then it and I came back to Earth, and some part of my mind grasped that my best wasn't good enough. I wrote and started drawing a story called "The Long Arm of the Telstar" but never finished it. The very last panel I drew showed the Telstar in an alley, surrounded by the Matador, the Bird of Prey, and the Victim, and thinking, "Uh-oh . . ."

But it wasn't just a sense of defeat that made me stop. *The Catcher in the Rye, The Graduate, The Sun Also Rises*, the fact that Oberlin had a writing program—all of it had been bubbling just beneath the surface of my consciousness. Then, one day in the spring of 1981, as I was walking to the bottom of Division Avenue for one of Ruff's Barber Shop's hit-or-miss haircuts, I thought about seeing what I could do with words alone.

In addition to my top choice, Oberlin, the other three schools I applied to—Georgetown, George Washington University, and Atlanta's Emory University—accepted me, too. I wanted to leave DC, and Emory offered me more money than Oberlin, so I felt obligated for Ma's sake to go there. Then came the Atlanta child murders, with a succession of black teenage boys in that city disappearing and later being found dead. Ma made the unilateral decision that I was not going anywhere near Atlanta, and I set my sights, once more, toward Ohio. Sometimes I think about the me in an alternate universe, the one who went to Emory, and I wonder where he went after that, and what he's doing now.

In the summer of 1981—as Phyllis, now married to Elliot, grew visibly pregnant with their first child—the me in this universe tried but failed to find a job. Instead, every morning I hopped in Wanda's little green Chevy Chevette and drove to the bottom of Division to run two miles on the track at Woodson Senior High. Back at 232 I sat on the back porch and drank coffee while reading Stanley Elkin novels. In the afternoons I hung out with Kev and, to a lesser extent, our friends Jeff Bryson and John Hill; we saw a few movies, including the new one everybody was talking about, *Raiders of the Lost Ark*. I loved Indiana Jones's mix of scholarship and physical feats, maybe because it reminded me of my cousin Billy's throwing the pistol over the roof while being able to spell "up." On TV that summer I saw Woody Allen's *Annie Hall*, a kind of comic take on the Holden Caulfield/Ben Braddock idea; I loved that, too.

And I wrote. That summer I turned out forty typed, single-spaced pages of very thinly disguised autobiography, my maiden attempt to take on the theme of the confused young man, the romantic outsider. The pages began: "It was hot, boy. Really hot. That sticky, sweaty, don't-stand-so-close-to-me hot." The story was well-written; it was also immature, self-indulgent, and boring, a work that was to literature what the Canary had been to comics. I didn't know that at the time, of course, and I'm not sure it would have mattered if I had. In my mind, I was already a writer.

Interlude

In tenth grade, for reasons that elude me now, I did something I had never done before and haven't since: join a sports team. I ran track. Kev joined, too; his long legs made him a pretty decent hurdler, and for a brief time he had the nickname "Reindeer." As for me, even on our ragtag team—which didn't so much as have uniforms, and which routinely lost meets against other schools—I didn't stand out. But I did run one race I'll never forget. The meet was at a school called St. John's; though it took place during late winter or early spring, when there was still a chill in the air, it was held outdoors. The relay race was run on a raised wooden track. I was the anchor, or the last of my team's four runners. This is how much better the other team was: in the time it took our first three guys to complete their runs, all four of St. John's runners finished. In other words, I was looking at running against nobody in a race my team had already lost. I assumed at first that I wouldn't have to do it. What would be the point? But then here came our third runner, Glenn Penn (I do not make this up), flying down the track in the home stretch of his run, his feet pounding the wood, shouting at me to start sprinting before he passed me the baton; here came shouts from our sandy-haired young coach, a priest-in-training, who was standing below; and off I went, baton in hand, carrying out the definition of a doomed mission.

Life, like a St. John's runner, goes by with bewildering speed, and I have spent far too much of mine comparing myself with other people; that is a mug's game, but one that is hard for most of us to avoid entirely. (My favorite passage from Plutarch's life of Julius Caesar is when he quotes the weeping general saying to his friends, "Do you not think it a cause for grief that Alexander at my age was already king of so many nations, and I as yet have accomplished nothing at all remarkable?") But once in a while a ray of wisdom pierces the clouds, and I remember the moments of my run in that relay race. As I began sprinting, it was embarrassment and the desire to get off that track as soon as possible that fueled my legs; but as I kept running, moving faster than I ever had in my life, my Afro blowing in the wind (so Kev later told me), our coach shouting up at me, "Go, Cliff, baby!," something else took over. I was no longer trying to avoid embarrassment; the focus was not on beating somebody else (that was, of course, out of the question now); I was simply focused on my own task, doing it as well as I could, without a thought for my place among others or for circumstances beyond my control.

College and Self-preservation

Oberlin, Ohio, is a small town, flat as a piece of paper, with no tall objects—natural or man-made—to slow the winds that sweep through during its bitterly cold winters. Its nearest neighboring city is Cleveland, thirty miles away; its commercial district consists of two blocks that meet at a right angle, beyond which are houses and farmland. The center of the town, and the biggest thing in it, is Oberlin College. The word "liberal" is to the college what "tall" is to the NBA. Founded in 1833, Oberlin was, as any piece of its literature will tell you, the first college in the country to admit women and blacks. Among its three thousand students, hippies, leftist activists, atheists, gay men, radical feminists, and lesbians all felt at home.

All of that was true, anyway, in the fall of 1981, the year I became one of Oberlin's two hundred or so black students. I had not yet arrived on campus when I made the first, fateful move of my college career. The summer before my freshman year, when I received housing information, I saw that there was a dorm called African Heritage House. When I think of that now, I imagine the reactions of other incoming black freshmen to seeing that there was a dorm with that name. Maybe some of them, coming from schools where there had been few blacks and seeking a grounding in their own culture, said, "That's where *I'm* going!" Maybe others did the same, reluctant to live around a lot of whites for different reasons—insecurity, or fear of prejudice, or the simple human desire to be with others of one's kind. Then there was me. I reasoned, naively, that a place called African Heritage House must be a place for *serious* students of African history (as opposed to black American history), which I was not. I wasn't worried about being alone as a black student; I figured that, in a place of higher learning in post–civil rights era America, most blacks would be, ha ha, scattered throughout the rest of the campus. And as for feeling grounded in blackness: what *else* had I been for eighteen years, coming from where I did? I chose a dorm called—rather appropriately—Fairchild, a smallish, three-story building where, somewhat to my surprise, I was one of only three black students and the sole black male. It didn't bother me. I simply interacted with the students who were physically closest to me. They were mostly white, of course. But if they didn't look like me, they were, for the most part, very friendly, and, except for the slight southern tinge to my voice that I didn't even know was there until I left DC, they *sounded* like me.

Occasionally there came a small sign of difference—beyond the obvious one—between me and those kids. One day, talking to a female student, I said something about James Brown. In a mildly puzzled tone, the young woman said, "I don't think I've ever *heard* of James Brown." I blinked at her. Bright, pretty, outgoing, funny, she didn't seem like someone whose parents had kept her locked in a closet before she came to college, so I couldn't make sense of what she'd just told me—which, where I'd come from, was the equivalent of, "I don't think I've ever *heard* of George Washington." But in this place I'd come *to*, as I gradually discovered, she was not alone.

The opposite of that exchange, you might say, took place at a let's-get-to-know-each-other party held in Fairchild's lounge by our dorm directors the first week of school. We played a game in which everyone had the name of a famous person taped to his or her back; we had to ask one another questions to figure out the names. The more students I talked to, and the more questions I asked, the further I seemed to get from the answer, until I broke down and asked somebody to please tell me what the hell was on my back. The answer: "C. S. Lewis." *Who?* Lewis, as I now know—having read his work aloud to my own children—was the author of the brilliant, classic young-adult novels in the Narnia Chronicles series. This, it seemed, was the kind of reading done in neighborhoods where kids routinely picked up books for fun, where no one asked, while looking at you as if an ear had grown out of your forehead, "Why you *read?*"

I took that kind of thing in stride. Harder to shrug off was the gap between what was expected of me as a student and what I was prepared to do. It's hard now to say for sure what I was thinking about schoolwork. I do remember my disappointment upon discovering that with few exceptions (of which I wasn't one) freshmen were not allowed in creative-writing classes. That left me with plain old academic coursework. Maybe I'd become so used to getting good grades with minimal effort that I expected to do the same at Oberlin; maybe I saw how much was being asked of me and didn't feel like working so hard for something as ho-hum as good grades had once been. Maybe one of those factors, or both, combined with a third, which is that I was simply having a good time. In my first week of college I learned to play poker; there was a set of chips in the dorm lounge, and pretty much any evening I seemed able to scare up three people to play a few hands at the round table in Fairchild's lounge, which involved much talking and laughing. Then there was the Rathskeller—the Rat—the low-lit student tavern with its heavy wooden furniture and tables, its steady roar of talk and laughter, its crowd of eighteen-to-twenty-two-year-olds in T-shirts and flannel and jeans, and its cheap, free-flowing 3.2-percent-alcohol beer, which I couldn't tell in those days from the real thing. I had never known such fun.

My classes were a different matter. In my first semester I took a course in Black American literature taught by the writer Calvin Hernton, one of the only classes in which I could count on knowing from one minute to the next what was going on. My one-credit government class seemed to be going well enough, until we took a test based on a book I hadn't even bothered to finish reading. (Under one of my answers the professor wrote, "Almost chemically pure bull.") A charismatic, widely loved professor named Hirschel Kasper taught my four-credit economics class, moving around at the bottom of that cavernous lecture hall like a seasoned actor giving a one-man show; Professor Kasper was fond of saying one thing I still remember—"If an idea is good in theory but not good in practice, then it's not good in theory"—but I've forgotten the rest of what he said, which is not surprising, since I couldn't decipher it even then. (Doing more of the reading might have helped.) I had a one-credit class in geology ("Rocks for Jocks"). Finally, there was the class I took, for some reason, on surrealism, taught in a hall as enormous as the one where I took econ. The professor was Sanford Shepard, an American whose ever-present tweed jacket and pipe gave him, for me, a European air. Of them all, this was the class that most made me feel I was watching a three-dimensional TV show, able to see and hear people who didn't seem to see me, even though I was the sole black student there, and who couldn't hear me, because I was too mystified to open my mouth. (And once again: if I'd read a few more of the books . . .)

I continued to enjoy myself outside class. One night a pillow fight broke out between the kids in my dorm and students from one a short distance away; it was so much fun that a day or so later I and a guy named Chris, the one student I knew who did less work than me, set out to organize another. Throughout the day we tried to enlist people for a raid that evening. "Sure, okay," they told us, but they were nowhere to be found when evening rolled around—except for one rather chubby girl, who saw Chris and me, ran to her room faster than I would have thought possible, and slammed the door. Chris and I were left standing, baffled and let-down, outside the open door of two female students, the frizzy-haired Sarah and the very straight-haired Melanie. And now came the first of two occasions during my college years when a young woman, with a handful of words, parted the clouds for me and let in the light. Melanie, who was my age, said to Chris and me, not without sympathy, "This isn't summer camp, guys."

Her words, which get some of the credit for saving my college career, came too late to salvage the semester. Never will I forget the day I went to the mailroom and pulled from box #2609 the envelope containing my grades. Holding it close to me—as if it were a small child threatening to shout the news of my stupidity to the world—I went to a secluded spot on the top floor of Mudd Library. Only there did I dare to look. The good news: I had done well in Black American Lit, managed a B- in Surrealism, and passed Geology (thanks to a very lenient grade on my final exam, at the bottom of which the professor wrote, "Merry Christmas"). The bad news: I had bombed Economics and Government—five credits in all, leaving me with seven for the semester, two short of the absolute minimum. I, Clifford Thompson, the darling of my teachers from kindergarten through twelfth grade, was on academic probation.

The reaction from 232 Division Avenue was not the explosion it could have been, considering that Ma was footing the bill for a college education I had treated more or less like a slumber party. My mother was less angry than concerned; she was satisfied when I promised I would do better. I wondered, as I was to wonder about a number of things, what my father would have said.

One day a year or so later I was in a dining hall with a couple of other students, who were discussing college work. They agreed with each other that if we couldn't handle the work now, we would never be able to. The truth of that statement seemed self-evident to me then; it seems suspect now. I had made a hash of my first college semester not because I was dumb (though I wondered at moments if that was true), and not because of my inadequate inner-city education, but because I was unmotivated. All I cared about was writing; otherwise, beyond the fear of failing and of everything that would follow from that, I didn't know why I was doing what I was doing. Today I have interests in world history and the history of literature, film, and art, subjects I wish to God I had cared about in the days when my only job was to learn. But if my first-semester fiasco didn't immediately awaken the intellectual in me, it gave the survivor a kick in the pants. I knew I had to get busy if I wanted to stay in college, and that's what I did, spending more time with my head bent over my lamplit desk, in that singular dorm-room quiet, as the sky outside my window grew black.

===

Meanwhile: dating.

I went out drinking, played poker, and ate breakfast, lunch, and dinner with white kids, but the thought of dating one seemed like something else again. It wasn't that my family had preached against dating across the color line; it was simply that I lacked an example. Other than Sidney Poitier and Katharine Houghton in *Guess Who's Coming to Dinner*, I didn't know of an interracial couple. Uncle Brock and Aunt Catherine's son Bill had married Yvonne, a white woman, but they didn't count as a couple, having been separated for as long as I could remember; I liked Bill and Yvonne (and their little daughter, Catherine), but an ad for black-white romance they were not. Hence my assumption that anyone I dated would be black—an assumption that ran so deep that I hadn't consciously considered any other possibility. Hence, also, my pursuit of one particular black woman who lived across campus: a pathetic campaign that lasted long after she'd made it clear that she had no interest in me. Then, sometime in the fall of 1981, I had a conversation with my (white) roommate. I made a comment implying that anyone I dated would be black; my roommate responded, "Who says you have to have a black girlfriend?" I don't remember my answer to that question. I didn't shout "My God, you're right!" and run out to kiss the first white female I saw. But by fall break of freshman year I had begun a long-term relationship with my first girlfriend, who was white.

I returned to 232 after seven weeks, by far the longest I'd ever been away from home; walking in, I thought everything in the house looked slightly out of place. In talking about school over the next few days, I told Wanda about my new girlfriend, and what color she was. My sister merely nodded. I started to tell Ma, but wasn't sure how, and in the end I didn't—she found out from Wanda and called me after I'd gone back to school, saying, "You didn't tell me she was white!" Ma wasn't upset and didn't disapprove; as with my grades, she was simply concerned—this mother of mine, who had brought three black children into the world before *Brown v. Board of Education*—and she told me, "Just be careful, hear?" This crossing of racial boundaries was all well and good, she seemed to be saying, but I needed to look out for myself, too.

The girlfriend in question, whom we'll call Joanne, was from Cleveland; she was a very smart science major with an innocently pretty face. Joanne was far from being a hippie but had features I associate with young hippie girls: long teeth, long, straight brown hair parted in the middle; she even had a hooded, off-white Mexican-style pullover sweater she liked to wear, the kind often seen on middle-class kids who dress poorer than they are. Joanne was very shy and quiet; it wasn't so much that she didn't talk as that when she did, at least in groups of people she didn't know well, you had to lean in to hear her. Her genuinely sweet nature had a cloudier side—those scars on her wrists were not, as she told me when we met, from broken glass—and she was capable of manipulation, which, along with my own irresoluteness, helps explain why we stayed together as long as we did. That said, I liked her a lot, and we had a tender relationship. Tender, and volatile. It is not an uncommon scenario: a boy and girl get together; one of them (in this case, me) likes the other but also feels the need to date more people; they break up tearfully but try to remain friends; continuing to spend time together, they're soon a couple again, though they may call it something else (I think our most creative term was "physical best friends"); and then they're back to the original problem. Repeat that four or five times, and you have the story of my romance with Joanne. I quote Norm from the sitcom *Cheers*, talking to Sam about Sam's relationship with Diane: "You're lovely, special people. *Alone. Separately.* You know, individually. Together, frankly, you stink." Poor Joanne at least had the excuse of being in love with me.

"Capable of manipulation": the example of this that I remember is a painful one to recount, which probably means that I ought to recount it. One day I said to Joanne that I'd been spending so much time with her that I thought Chris might feel neglected. "Would you be upset," I asked her, "if I went to the movies with Chris tonight?" The movie was *Annie Hall*. "No," she said, "but I'll be upset if you don't ask me to go with you." Chris agreed to go to the movies with us. Then he found out there was a poker game going on; he wanted to play, and so did I. When I said as much to Joanne, she was indignant, because I'd promised to go to the movies with her. So while Chris played poker, I went to *Annie Hall* with Joanne, spending most of the two hours checking my watch, hoping the game would still be going when the movie was over. I not only missed the poker game; I had to hear Joanne's complaints about how distracted I'd been while I was with her.

The situation, of course, called—begged—for me to say to Joanne, *Look. I told you I wanted to spend an evening with my friend. We want to play poker. If you can't handle one evening without me, that's not my problem.* But I was dealing with a woman who as a teen had been diagnosed as schizophrenic, who had spent some time in a mental hospital, who had demonstrated what she could do if she felt bad enough; my knowing this, and her knowing that I knew it, gave her power over me, which she maintained by using it just often enough.

You may be wondering how I can describe this same person as having a "genuinely sweet nature," and yet she did. When she wasn't making me feel guilty and boxed-in, Joanne made me feel that I was attractive; that my gentleness was a virtue, not a weakness; that I was not—as I feared—simply too stupid to succeed at Oberlin; that I could do well if I tried hard enough. Joanne was proof of how many things one personality can encompass. And didn't this poor damaged girl need a friend (even if I was, in a way, the worst kind she could have)? Hadn't my family always taken care of my grandmother, who couldn't make it without us?

84

At the start of sophomore year Joanne transferred to the University of Cincinnati—to get away from me after one too many breakups, if memory serves. I now lived in a different dorm at Oberlin, which is how I got to be friends with two black male students, Jamil and Tracy. Jamil, a friendly, talkative freshman from the DC area, had the room next to mine; he got to be tight with Tracy, a tall, equally talkative sophomore I had met the year before, and so I did, too. Tracy lived at African Heritage House, and for the first time I went there on a regular basis, often at mealtimes, the three of us—those two chatterboxes and me—eating with others at large round tables. From my Black Lit classes the year before I had known some of the students at African Heritage House to say "hi" to; there were others I met for the first time. Many were friendly to me, and all were at least civil. But Jamil and Tracy told me things they said about me when I wasn't around: "You *know* he went out with somebody *white* last year"; "I'm glad to see him hanging with some brothers for a change." Whereas I had been on academic probation the year before, I had the feeling now that I was on racial probation. I didn't like that a bit.

Joanne returned to Oberlin in the spring of sophomore year. I was glad to see her. We began to spend time together as, ho ho, friends, and then one thing led to another. African Heritage House (except for Tracy, who's still my friend) washed its hands of me at that point.

Then *I* went away. By that time I had gotten my act together enough to apply successfully to the Oberlin-in-London program, and at the start of my junior year I made my first trip across the Atlantic. I'll never forget walking out of Heathrow Airport, seeing those enormous black taxis, hearing the accent of my driver, and feeling like I'd stepped into an old film.

I returned from that theater-focused London semester with my trunk, a big black diary I'd begun keeping, an inflated sense of my critical powers, and a determination that I would not get romantically involved with Joanne again. Naturally, then, the very night that my trunk and diary and I made it back to campus, I slept with her; as I recall it, I felt the warmth of her hand on the back of my neck, and I was done for. Our dating-in-everything-but-name continued for a time.

One Saturday morning, the morning of my twenty-first birthday,

Joanne and I were in my dorm room, a single. We made love, and then we had one of our tortured conversations; I said, once again, that I wanted to be free to date other people, and she wept at these words, as if hearing them for the first time and not the twelfth. When she had calmed down, I left for my shift at whatever food-service job I had then. Joanne stayed behind in my room; I forget the reason she gave.

She was gone when I came back, but I found a short letter from her. This furious—make that venomous—note, unlike any communication we'd ever had, shocked me. It also confused me. Was the note a delayed reaction to what I'd said, which she'd heard before? Was it frustration that had accumulated over the course of our relationship and exploded, for some reason, on my birthday? None of that added up, which made me wonder, just for a moment, if—but no, that couldn't be what had happened, if only because it was too horrifying to contemplate.

But that was *exactly* what had happened. As Joanne confirmed later, in a second note even more vitriolic than the first, she had read my diary. In essence there was nothing in those pages that she hadn't heard from my own lips, but things were spelled out, literally, in detail that must have been excruciating for her to read. And that, as she wrote to me, was the reason she'd picked up the diary: for the "jolt" that would do what neither of us seemed capable of doing otherwise—namely, ending our relationship. It worked. Our romance, our not-dating, our physical-best-friendship, our whatever-you-want-to-call-it, was dead.

Now *I* was angry. I felt violated, indignant, sad, depressed, guilty, and, amidst all that, however obscurely in the beginning, liberated. I was free of this unhealthy relationship—free, black, and twenty-one.

A week later I darted down to DC for Grandma's ninetieth birthday party, and I was back in DC again for spring break the week after that, by which time Grandma was sick. When a ninety-year-old woman has a fever and can't hold down her food, everyone thinks what no one wants to say, and the fear of mine that had never been buried very deeply was now at the surface. I was afraid that I wouldn't be able to handle what had to happen eventually: the death of the grandmother who loved me so dearly, whom I teased incessantly as the only way I knew to express the love I felt in return. I thought of the "Love, Grandmother" written in big, shaky letters in my birthday cards; I thought of her saying to me long-distance, "HI! THIS IS GRANDMA"—as if that voice could have been anyone else's—while holding the phone, so Ma said, out in front of her face. She was still sick when I returned to school. Between that and the situation with Joanne, I must have looked like I was trying out for the lead in *Hamlet*, because two good friends of mine—Donna May and my London-semester pal Charles Hawley—suggested independently of each other that I visit Psych Services.

Then Grandma got better. Spring came to Oberlin, that season when the very air we breathed was warm with possibility, with all those young bodies suddenly outside—that season I will always associate with my college days. The leaves returned, and the gray-brown look and feel of the campus gave way to a vibrant green; the temperature rose, and my spirits rose with it. And instead of going to Psych Services, I went on dates.

We come now to the second time that I was enlightened by a few perfectly chosen words from a young woman. I was out for the evening with Victoria; having already made it to first base with this rather glamorous blond, I was feeling relaxed, and I settled into Thompson mode—meaning that when she asked, "What do you want to do now?" I answered with some variation on, "I don't care. Whatever you'd like." We were strolling in the moonlight, in the balmy April air, when I made that response for maybe the third time. Victoria stopped walking, stood in front of me, and gently took hold of my shirt; looking into my eyes with a broad, dazzling smile that represented the very last of her patience, she said, "Make . . . a decision."

Those three words sank in very slowly, in the end speaking volumes to me—much more than Victoria could possibly have intended. *Make . . . a decision*: the other person does not have to, and should not always, decide for you; you count, too; you can be a nice guy and still express your wishes; you have to find a balance between taking care of others and taking care of yourself.

Interlude

At Oberlin I wrote fiction—constantly—for my classes and for myself, all of it being the same to me. Oberlin's Creative Writing Department was run then by a poet, Stuart Friebert, a fiftyish, tall, gangly man with glasses and short-cropped, graying hair. Stuart had a gentle, even self-effacing manner that I came to discover was like a fuzzy blanket thrown over a brick post. A story I heard—and had no trouble believing—was that one earnest young man submitted a piece of writing to Stuart and demanded to know everything that was wrong with it. Stuart's reply, which I can imagine him delivering in his hushed tone, like a literary Mafia don, was reported to be: "If I told you everything that's wrong with this, you'd never write again." A professor of German by training, Stuart had started the Creative Writing Department with his wife, Diane Vreuls, a fiction writer, more than a decade earlier; he seemed to have read everything ever published, and over the years he had developed his own vocabulary for discussing student work. "It's a good cartoon," he might say about a story; "It's a bad cartoon," would be his judgment on another. "That word weighs a *ton* in English," I remember him telling me once, though I've forgotten which very heavy word I had used. Some of his comments were much easier to interpret; his favorite word to write alongside a stanza or paragraph was "Ugh," and a friend of mine got a poem back with "Yikes!" on it. Where my work was concerned, Stuart was an expert at giving encouragement one moment and taking nearly all of it back the next, leaving me with just enough to stagger forward. "You have a good prose gift," he told me one day, "which will take a long time to develop."

===

My Oberlin girlfriend Rebecca Bigler didn't get along with her roommate. For that reason, which she later admitted was an excuse, she moved into my little single with me, Room 236 of Noah Hall, with its sky-blue walls and view out the window of the visiting fiction writer Mary Robison's house across the street.

Rebecca was a quiet but extremely driven psychology major (she has gone on to renown in that field) with long, dark, wild hair and long painted nails. That hair—sometimes she would shove a comb in to hold it in place; I almost felt sorry for that comb, which was like a lone, unarmed deputy sent to restore order in a Dodge City saloon exploding with punches, smashed bottles, and flying chairs. Rebecca and I laughed the day we discovered that our driver's licenses had us both at five feet eight inches and a hundred and forty pounds. The Minnesota-born Rebecca loved to dance—she told me early on that as kids, she and her sister had watched *Soul Train* "to learn to dance like black people"—and I probably spent more nights in the disco the first semester of my senior year than in the three previous years combined. And she was an ardent feminist. I would classify the views I'd had on male-female relations up until then as rudimentary feminism; in high school I had once argued vehemently with a male physics teacher who thought women's jobs were to cook, clean, and have babies (a stance for which I was thanked afterward by being called a "froot loop" by the one girl in the class). But Rebecca lent my views clarity and sophistication. On campus we went to see the movie *Tender Mercies*, which starred Robert Duvall as a country singer who is down and out at the beginning of the story but proceeds to pull himself together—I recall it as the one movie I've ever seen that had no discernible conflict. The conflict was supplied by Rebecca, who complained about a song the Duvall character had sung, called something like "You Hold the Ladder," with "you" being the singer's wife. "It's more of that 'Stand by Your Man' bullshit," Rebecca said after it was over. "Hold your own goddamn ladder!" Rebecca, whose father was a painter, also turned my attention for the first time to non-comics-related art—mostly the work of the Impressionists. I yakked to her about various interests of mine, and I was excited one day to read in the local TV listings that *Cooley High* would be on late that night. Rebecca and I huddled up in her dorm room and watched, and I think we were equally disappointed—she because of all she'd heard about the movie from me, I because nothing in my loving memory had hinted at what an amateurish film *Cooley High* is in a lot of ways. (Glynn Turman was still great as Preach, though.)

Between us Rebecca and I had maybe a half-dozen records that we played over and over and over again and somehow didn't get sick of. There was her Bruce Springsteen tape (*Born in the USA*), Prince tape (*Purple Rain*), and Bob Dylan tape (I forget, but it had the hilarious "Bear Mountain Blues" on it); there was my Talking Heads LP (*Remain in Light*, which I never even bothered to flip over to the second side) and my Beethoven albums, Symphony no. 6 and Symphony no. 7. We laughed over the fact that I liked the Talking Heads, those art-rock darlings of tie-dyed young whites, while Rebecca, who was white, liked Prince, whose picture had graced many a girl's locker in my nearly all-black high school.

The Beethoven albums, which I'd bought during the summer of 1984, represented my decision to hear some classical music. Other than what I'd played in the DCYO program, they were the first pieces of wordless music I listened to. Because I played Symphony no. 6—The Pastoral—so often beginning in that fall, as the air turned crisp on the still-green Oberlin campus, it will always make me think of new seasons, new beginnings. Both symphonies led me to realize that music could embrace themes, even tell stories, without words. I wondered, I wonder still, how much Beethoven intended of what I heard. Late in the first movement of Symphony no. 7, for example, there is a passage that begins with an oboe solo, which evokes innocence; as the poignant passage continues, slipping for two measures or so into a minor key, it sounds to me absolutely like innocence learning new truths, some of them dark, their totality bringing on successive moods of excitement, bewilderment, anger, and, finally, mature acceptance—about ten bars of music, describing the stages of a human life.

===

I graduated from Oberlin in 1985 and went back to DC, living at 232 while I applied to grad programs in creative writing—a total of three schools, two of them among the most competitive in the country, the third a "safety" school I didn't even want to attend. I wonder now what I was using for brains during that process.

While applying I landed a job in Georgetown as an editorial assistant at a little place called Carroll Publishing. My boss and co-workers, four white women in all, were nice; the office, with red interior brick, many shops nearby, and a view of the tour boats on the C&O Canal, was lovely; the work we did revealed previously unexplored possibilities of boredom. Carroll published directories of federal, county, and municipal government officials—glorified telephone books. Our jobs were to maintain the databases from which the directories were drawn, which often meant calling up poor unsuspecting people all over the country and pumping them for information about their colleagues' titles and phone numbers. One afternoon a woman I was talking to suddenly said, "Hello?"—which was how I realized that in the middle of our conversation I had fallen asleep. To relieve the tedium my co-workers and I sometimes called out to each other names we'd come across. (My personal favorite: Glen Ifuku.) One day my boss, Nancy, said, "Listen to this one: Bland Brockenborough." To which I replied, "He's my cousin."

If I didn't feel I'd reached the pinnacle of professional success, Grandma was proud of her young working man. Every single morning of the nine months I spent at Carroll, my grandmother, ninety-one years old, made me breakfast before I headed off to the Metro. An image from my first morning of work is stamped indelibly on my mind: a view from the bottom of the stairs of my grandmother standing in the kitchen, wearing a headscarf and blue apron, lips curled in with the effort of stirring batter for the pancakes she was cooking for me.

===

The December after I graduated from college, I went to see a movie—*Young Sherlock Holmes*—with my high-school buddy John Hill and his girlfriend. I was sitting in the theater, drinking a Coke, when it happened: my heartbeat seemed to stop, and then, a moment later, it resumed, with what seemed to be three times its usual force. I was alarmed but did nothing, said nothing, hoping it was a weird one-time occurrence. Then, over the following days and weeks, it happened more, usually when I was at rest. The logical thing to do, of course, would have been to see a doctor, or at least tell a family member. I did neither. I acted—or didn't act—partly out of the old stoicism from the Marvin Henderson days of a decade earlier, the do-it-aloneism of my childhood; I was also afraid. My father had died eleven years before of a heart attack. I didn't want to be told that the same would happen to me. So I acted like nothing was wrong. Everything was fine.

===

I kept writing, starting to send stories out to literary magazines. There were two kinds of responses: the form letter and the variation on "This is accomplished in many ways, but in the end we didn't feel that" blah blah etc. For a while I had quite a correspondence going with C. Michael Curtis, an editor at *The Atlantic*, who would turn down one of my stories with a letter that encouraged me to send more, then say no to that one with an equally nice note, and so on, in a kind of repeating mirror image of rejection.

===

Living at 232 again had meant being back in the old neighborhood, which many of my junior high classmates had never left, and from time to time I ran into one or another of them. In my last school memory of Robbin Craw-ford, he and I had been in the locker room, where I had thrown a shirt at his head in response to something else and he had mentioned throwing a punch. But we were in our early twenties the day I saw him on the street and he greeted me with, "How you be?"—the big smile on his very dark face making it seem that he really wanted to know. Another time I saw Darryl Woodward (not to be confused with Big Darryl or Little Darryl), who to my astonishment ended our conversation by saying sincerely, "It's good to see you."

　　Then there was the day when, walking home from the Metro, I found myself in step with Tyrone Hare. With Robbin and Darryl I had had brief exchanges, but my walk with Tyrone represented the first real conversation I'd had with one of these guys in years. In junior high Tyrone had been my chief nemesis on the sexual front—teasing me every day about my virginity—just as Marvin Henderson had headed up the violence department. Now, though, Tyrone was asking me pleasantly what I had been doing with myself. I answered him with an edge in my voice that said, *What's it to you?* Seeming not to pick up on this, he asked what I had studied in college. "English and creative writing," I told him, in the same, just-short-of-rude tone. "That's you," he said with a friendly smile.

Even before the conversation ended, I began to feel a little guilty. A decade earlier, in the thick of my junior-high misery, I had found meager solace in the thought that I was a better, more mature person than my tormentors; but in my talk with Tyrone, who had seemed the mature one, and who had acted like the boy of twelve? Seeing Tyrone was like water on the seeds that had been planted by Robbin Crawford and Darryl Woodward. Slowly, those junior high years began the process of transforming in my mind, of seeming just a little less like a time of unforgivably bad behavior and more like a long, dismal costume party, in which we boys had come as people struggling to square our changing bodies with our true selves. Tyrone and most of the others, it seemed, had taken off their disguises; maybe, just maybe, it was time I thought about stepping out of the role of resentful victim. Leaving Tyrone, I took a step away from my childhood, even as I headed back to 232.

===

In the spring of 1986, after a two-week stretch that saw my grad-school plans and my long-distance romance with Rebecca crash and burn, I got two helpful pieces of advice. Wanda's was that I give myself a short time to wallow in my misery and then start figuring out what I would do next. My Oberlin friend Donna May, who was living in DC at the time, referred to a passage in a novel we were both reading then, Jay McInerney's *Ransom*. At one point the title character, a young American martial-arts student in Japan, has a sparring match with a better and more seasoned fighter; after several minutes of getting his ass kicked, Ransom channels his frustration and pain—from both inside and outside the dojo—into a beautifully executed kick that lands squarely in the middle of the other man's chest. Donna's idea was that I try to do the same thing: convert the pain of rejection from various corners into some kind of bold move. (At the end of the novel Ransom is all but decapitated with a sword, but Donna didn't dwell on that part.)

I tried to take Wanda and Donna up on their advice, announcing to Ma one Saturday that I was going downtown to Martin Luther King Library "to look up my future." And that was how I made it to New York.

The Apple and Mrs. O.

I had heard that she worked there, but that seemed like a myth, barely more believable than accounts of UFO sightings. Then one day I rounded the corner to the 43rd-floor elevators, and there she was, seeming to have stepped out of one of her pictures. She stood alone among a half-dozen or so other people, with the expression one has at such times, the gaze of mild concern at something that wasn't there. Hoping for some sign of confirmation, I studied the other people around me, but they looked neither at one another nor back at me. An elevator came, heading down, and a few people got on, chatting in normal tones. This, it seemed, was par for the course, as it soon became for me, too: just another afternoon of working at the Doubleday book-publishing company alongside Jacqueline Kennedy Onassis.

If I have a vague memory today of what I thought back then—how I imagined publishing companies operated, or why I wanted to work for one—it's probably because my thinking at the time was pretty vague, too. I wanted to be a writer, and so I had moved to New York and sought a job having to do with books, an idea that made sense as long as you didn't consider it too long. I hadn't yet read anything by John Irving, but I had seen the movie version of his novel *The World According to Garp*, in which the young Garp and his mother take it into their heads to write books and then, next thing you know, are alone in a meeting with the head of a publishing company. The political equivalent of that scene might be one in which a bus driver, having decided to become secretary of state, strolls into the White House and has a heart-to-heart chat with the president. I didn't know that then, though, and my conception of the day-to-day operation of a publishing house probably had comparable elements of fantasy. I think I pictured something like this: an editor in a rumpled tweed jacket or sweater with patched elbows sits in an office whose walls are covered with black-and-white photos of Scott and Zelda Fitzgerald, Ford Madox Ford, Gertrude Stein; he spends the morning there, sipping cup after cup of black coffee while perusing manuscripts that have come in, taking the measure of the writers' way with a metaphor, judging the beauty of the sentences. Around eleven-thirty his assistant (me), who has been at the same task at a desk outside the editor's office, comes in to compare notes, the two of them digressing into a general discussion of literature that takes them up to lunch-time at a neighborhood restaurant crawling with literary types. Then it was back to the office at two or so, just buzzed enough on red wine or martinis to enhance the old creative powers for editing, the sun streaming through the office blinds onto the manuscript page—until about six, when it's time to meet friends at a nearby bar, elbows on the wood, shouting to be heard during the discussion of Dreiser.

It took a while for reality to intrude on that image. Doubleday, which then occupied four floors of a building on Park Avenue, had hired me without really knowing what to do with me—there weren't any entry-level openings in editorial that summer—so I started as what they called a floater, one who helped out in different departments as needed. For three months I worked in Legal, which was then negotiating Doubleday's sale of the New York Mets; for a stretch I put in twelve-hour days, typing contracts and the like. (I was working there the first time I saw Jackie O.)

Doubleday was yet another environment in which I found myself among very few black people, but one of them made a point of meeting the others. The thirty-something, mustached, just-short-of-portly editor Gerald Gladney already knew my name and which department I worked in the day he introduced himself to me in the hall. That day or soon afterward, he invited me to lunch, and I quickly learned a couple of things about him—one of them before we even made it to the restaurant: I started asking him something or telling him something about myself, and he said, "Let's wait until we sit down. Otherwise we might run out of conversation." At the restaurant, for some reason, I mentioned a (black) woman I'd liked in college who didn't give me the time of day, and Gerald said, "Because you're boring?"

(I reminded him of that question a couple of years later. It was the only time I ever saw him look embarrassed.) For reasons I've forgotten we got onto the subject of interracial dating, of which he seemed to disapprove. "I won't tell you what I did the other night, then," I said, alluding to a young white woman whom I had known at Oberlin, discovered was in New York, met for dinner in Manhattan, and, quite unexpectedly, accompanied to bed the same evening. "I don't care who you sleep with," Gerald said, with a look that suggested otherwise.

All of that makes Gerald sound mean, humorless, and self-righteous. He was none of those things. Well, he could be a little self-righteous. And occasionally a bit mean. But it turned out to be easy to get a belly laugh out of him, and if some of his comments carried a sting, he would also do anything for you if (1) he liked you and (2) you were black, and you didn't always have to be.

I appeared to meet those criteria, and he made an effort to make me known around the company. He advised me to attend an after-work book-publishing party—I forget whose book it was—held in a reception room at a fancy-schmancy hotel near Doubleday. Arriving before Gerald, and knowing exactly nobody, I introduced myself to the wine. I already had a nice buzz going when Gerald showed up and began taking me around. One person he introduced me to was a Doubleday executive editor named Loretta Barrett. The tall, white, dark-haired, fiftyish Loretta was one of those people whose amiability ("Oh, just call me Retta") was about as deep as her mascara—and came off more easily. (I was later to meet a female former assistant of hers. Typing Loretta's correspondence, and adding her boss's title at the close of each letter, this terrorized young woman had frequently made the Freudian slip of "Executive Idiot.") Loretta was the editor of a forthcoming book called *The Sexual Mountain and Black Women Writers*, by Calvin Hernton; Gerald informed her that Calvin had been one of my professors at Oberlin. Loretta then said to me, "He's wonderful! He really gives a lot of support to black feminists."

"Yeah," I said, smiling, full of wine. "*Both* of 'em!"

With that, the pleasantries were over. Loretta had her hands on her hips and a scowl on her face, and had gotten as far as "It's because of black men like you—" when Gerald whisked me away.

In that smooth-as-silk fashion I finally landed a spot as an editorial assistant in Anchor Press, the *serious* arm of Doubleday, which published high-toned original works and paperback versions of hardcover books from other houses. Anchor consisted of three other people—an assistant editor, an associate editor, and the executive editor and boss, the man I did most of my work for: Marshall De Bruhl. (Marshall wore *not* rumpled sweaters but very expensive-looking suits, white shirts, and ties.) Thus, twelve years after I had last seen my father, was I proven right: he hadn't died after all. He had merely gone to New York to become a book editor. Oh, someone else might have been fooled by details—say, the fact that Marshall was bald on top, whereas my father had a full head of hair; or that Marshall was fifty-one, whereas my father would now have been sixty-five; or that Marshall had a gray-white beard, whereas my father had never been able to grow one; or that Marshall's North Carolina accent was much more pronounced than my father's light Virginia twang; or that Marshall was Caucasian. But I knew the truth, because our relationship took up where it had left off. Marshall had a good, somewhat devilish, sometimes silly sense of humor and an endearing habit of laughing at his own jokes. He was also one of the more impatient people I have ever met, and he wasn't joking at all the day he told me, "Don't make mistakes. I don't like them."

At the time, unfortunately, mistakes were a kind of specialty of mine. I was twenty-three. Over the years I've observed that many males in their early twenties have a spaciness about them; I was to see it in quite a few young men I would supervise. It has little to do with intelligence, since a lot of these young men are very smart and have four years of college under their belts, and everything to do with where their minds are. They're thinking about how and when they're going to ask some young woman out, or about what they're going to say to interviewers in two years, when they publish their critically acclaimed first novels, or about what they're doing this weekend—about anything, in short, except the tasks in front of them. I was no exception to that general rule, and I was, it has to be said, a rather lousy editorial assistant, a job that did not correspond to the idea I'd had of it, which could be said of book publishing in general. I saw the editors do a variety of things during the workday: attend what were called focus meetings and pre-focus meetings, go to lunch with authors or literary agents, talk on the phone, yell at their assistants. What I never saw any of them do, even once, was edit. Something so secondary to the functioning of a book company, it seemed, was best done after hours, at home. The same was true of evaluating the books and manuscripts sent by agents—to say nothing of the never-looked-at "slush pile" of unsolicited submissions (which is where Garp's book would have ended up, right on top of his mother's). One day I heard Anchor's assistant editor, Ceci Scott, say without irony—in what I thought an extraordinary comment from an employee of a publishing house—"Who's got time to *read*."

For the barely paid editorial assistants, meanwhile, there were letters to type, short-tempered authors to deal with on the phone, and forms, forms, and more forms to fill out, forms whose connection to the shaping of great literature I couldn't make out. That brings me back to my lousiness as an assistant. "Can I ask you something, straight out?" Marshall said to me one day, holding a form related to back-cover text. "Why did you fuck this up? You're too *smart*." That last part is important in understanding why, in spite of everything, Marshall actually did like me. Another editor told me that Marshall said my written evaluations of book and manuscript submissions were "the best reports in the company." One of them, on a book forecasting economic trends in the near future, concluded, "It is hard enough, it seems to me, to write a good, coherent work on present-day realities. Predictions are especially tricky. Whether or not this one proves to be accurate, in five or eight years no one will care, which, I think, eliminates it from consideration." The reason I remember those lines, beyond the fact that I'm weird, is that Marshall was holding that report when he smiled over at me and said, "You really do write good reports, do you know that?"

As for those short-tempered authors, the phone call I remember best came from John Knowles. In those high-school years when I had truly begun reading novels, Knowles's *A Separate Peace* was behind only *The Catcher in the Rye* as my favorite, which is what made my exchange with him so disappointing. Marshall had talked to Knowles about the novelist's possibly writing a memoir. In a sign of how ill-fated an idea this was, Knowles turned to Marshall for inspiration, sending him hardcover copies of books he'd written (none of them nearly as successful as *A Separate Peace*) so that Marshall could get ideas for themes Knowles might tackle in the new work;

now that I think about it, I even wrote up a single-spaced page about my take on *A Separate Peace*. Marshall took a while to get to those volumes, if he ever did—hence Knowles's call. "I've got a question about my books," he said to me, Marshall having gone off to a meeting, or something. "Where the *fuck* are they?" I said, "I don't know, but I don't appreciate being talked to that way." Knowles replied, "I don't give a *fuck*"—at which point I hung up. After talking to him later, Marshall left a handwritten note on my chair: "John Knowles is full of contrition. Among other things, he's sorry."

Other encounters with the famous were more positive. Chinua Achebe, whose novel *Anthills of the Savannah* Anchor published, told a Doubleday publicist that I was very pleasant to talk to. Then there was Jacqueline Onassis, who was, to the (admittedly very limited) extent that I got to know her, graciousness itself. In the nineteen months I worked at Anchor, we moved offices three times, from the 39th floor to the 42nd floor to the 38th floor and finally, along with the rest of the company, from Park Avenue to 666 Fifth; as a result of that last move, my desk was maybe fifteen feet from Mrs. Onassis's office. (She came in Tuesday through Thursday, nine to noon. Good work if you can get it.) One day when both she and her assistant, my friend Judy Sandman, were out of the office, I answered her phone, which rang nearly nonstop. A couple of days later Jackie brought me a box of chocolates. (I ate the chocolates. I still have the box.) At the time the woman who sat at the desk behind mine was Gloria Muzio, an editorial assistant by day and theatrical director by night (today she has an impressive list of TV-directing credits). One day Gloria came in with a photograph of herself taken at the Sundance Film Festival; next to her in the photo was Robert Redford. I was admiring the photo when Jackie came down the hall. "Hey, Jackie," I said, "look at this," and I handed her the picture. Jackie— probably the most recognizable woman in the world, the widow of our most fondly remembered president, an international icon of style and grace— resembled a star-struck teenager as she said, "Oh, *my!*"

By then I was used to interacting with her and was un-awed in her presence, but that was not always the case. My first interaction with her took place one morning when she came to Marshall's office for a meeting with an author; I was dispatched to the cafeteria to get coffee for everyone, and when I returned I was unaware that I had one too many cups. I was back at my desk when Marshall's door opened and Mrs. Onassis came out holding a cup, which she brought over to where I sat, smiling and saying warmly, "Cliff, would you like this?" Somehow I forgot the punch line to this story until more than a dozen years later. After a long period of being out of touch, Marshall and I talked over the phone. "After the meeting," Marshall reminded me, "I went over to your desk and said, 'Well, now you can call your mother and tell her that Jackie Onassis served you coffee.' You said, 'I already did.'"

Interlude

My first December in New York, one of my fellow editorial assistants, a woman named Anne, invited the lot of us to a Christmas-tree-trimming party at her apartment in Hoboken. While there we watched the TV special *A Charlie Brown Christmas*, a staple of all our childhoods. One young woman there said to me about the character Linus, "He can take care of himself, but he's compassionate, too." She concluded with a nod, "Someone to emulate." (The woman rhapsodizing about Linus was named Lucy.) About a year later, still at Doubleday, I talked to another woman about *A Charlie Brown Christmas*, saying that I loved its music and wondered (this was years before Google) who had composed it. "Vince Guaraldi," she told me.

Thus did I spend a few dollars of my meager wages on a cassette, *Vince Guaraldi: Greatest Hits*, which I guess I have to call my first jazz record. Only a couple of tracks on that gem of an album are from *Charlie Brown*; the rest are straight-ahead jazz tunes, a couple with a Latin flavor, played by Guaraldi on piano and various others on bass and drums. One of its tracks, in particular, reminds me of that period of my life. "Manha de Carnaval" has an eight-bar theme—spare, linear, haunting right-hand piano lines that alternate with slower, lower tones from the left hand. The effect is of honest statements affirmed by shakes of the head that say, *Sad, but true*. There is a somberness about it—one that calls to my mind the bare tree limbs I could see from the window of my Brooklyn apartment, silhouetted against a cloudy sky at nightfall. But the tune has a loveliness, too. Hearing it at age twenty-four, I imagined having strong drinks with someone older, wiser, someone who would talk to me frankly about my life, offering no illusions, promising nothing, but pointing to a small number of real reasons for hope.

Listening to that music on nights when I was lonely, sick of my job, tired of my boss, mystified over my funky heartbeat, unsure of what I was doing in this city or with my life, I had the dim sense—the blessing of youth—that things would get brighter.

Writing, Race, and James Baldwin

During my three months in Doubleday's legal department, I worked mainly for Chris Goff, a tall, friendly, thirty-four-year-old Harvard Law grad born and raised in Virginia. One slow workday, Chris told me a story about his high-school years. It seems he drove a buddy of his and the buddy's pregnant girlfriend to North Carolina, where they would be able to get married without their parents' consent. When they got to the courthouse, the girl-friend—"showing the wisdom and foresight of a mountain high-school girl who would let my friend put her in that fix to begin with," as Chris phrased it to me recently—realized she had forgotten her ID. During the drive back home, Chris's still-unmarried buddy, bored, took out a pistol and shot holes in the road signs they passed. Impressed by this tale, I wrote a fictionalized account of it from various characters' points of view.

It was that short story that I handed, not without trepidation, to the truthful-to-a-fault Gerald Gladney when he asked to see something I had written. A day or two later I returned from lunch to find on my chair a page-long, typed, single-spaced note from Gerald that began, "Wow! You are good." Gerald soon set up a lunch meeting with the two of us and his own mentor, a black former Doubleday editor turned literary agent named Marie Brown. During the lunch I was at war with myself, wanting to make this all lead somewhere but afraid of putting my foot in my mouth; the result was that I talked in a very indirect way about what I wanted. At one point Gerald laughed and said, "My boy's so nervous." Then he asked Marie, "Are you hearing this? The boy wants his name in print." Marie was to help a little with that, though not for a while yet.

Meanwhile: in those years Doubleday used the services of a consultant named Gloria Jones, the novelist James Jones's widow, who was very friendly with Marshall. One day Marshall told me something about her that I didn't know how to take: that in that iconic photo of Marilyn Monroe standing over a sidewalk grate, with air lifting her dress to reveal very shapely legs, the legs had been those of Mrs. Jones. I found that difficult to believe, not only because (a) It was hard to picture the now-sixtyish Mrs. Jones as having legs anyone would want to photograph, but because (b) What could possibly have been wrong with Marilyn Monroe's legs? On the other hand, why would Marshall make up such a thing? To get someone else's take on this, I told my friend and fellow editorial assistant Keith Dawson what Marshall had told me. Keith's response reflected none of my confusion: "And my dad's Mario Cuomo!"

What *was* definitely true was that decades earlier, James and Gloria Jones had spent years in Paris, during which they were pals of James Baldwin—who died in November 1987, while I was at Doubleday. I was at my desk one morning when Marshall arrived at the office and informed me that Baldwin's funeral would take place at Manhattan's Cathedral of St. John the Divine. "You and I are going," he said. And that's what happened: On the gray day of the service, showing up at work in the one suit I owned, I got picked up by limo along with Marshall, and the two of us rode with Mrs. Jones to that magnificent cathedral. Sitting there with many others, including some of the brightest lights in contemporary literature, we listened to tributes from Maya Angelou, Amiri Baraka, and Toni Morrison. One of many sad things about the service was how much was wasted on me—a chuckleheaded twenty-four-year-old who, for all his supposed love of books, had barely read any Baldwin at all. Even worse, the funeral didn't inspire me to devour his collected works.

What did inspire me was a gift from Gerald. By then Doubleday had become part of Bantam Doubleday Dell; its imprint Laurel came out with paperback editions of Baldwin's books. Some time after Baldwin's funeral, Gerald came by my desk with a dozen of them. I dutifully took them home, where for a while they gathered dust. Man, did that change.

===

It was now 1988, the year I hit the quarter-century mark. Once again, things were brewing in my brain.

Several times a year I visited Division Avenue, which was changing. Uncle Manson and Uncle Nay were now widowers; Aunt Lucy had passed away in 1982, Aunt Emma in 1987. The 232 household had grown, though: Phyllis, married but living apart from Elliot (who was in medical school in the Dominican Republic), had moved back home with her two little girls, Emily and Elinor, in tow. That meant the house was home to not three but four generations. Grandma was still going at ninety-four, rising in the dark to make butter-soaked toast and have coffee with her sugar; Ma was happily retired from the post office, still—at sixty-four—taking care of her mother but sneaking off to her beloved Atlantic City with her buddy Martha when she could. While in DC I would catch up with my (black) friends: Jeff Bryson, another Youth Orchestra Program veteran, who was intrigued by the old records in the basement of 232 and today is the most knowledgeable person I know when it comes to soul music; my high school friend John Hill, who went over the years from short, skinny, shy if acerbic kid to muscular, quietly confident military man; our sassy high-school friend Kimberly Settle; and my ace boon coon, good old Kev.

Back in New York, though, except for the times I caught movies with Gerald, the people in my world—my friends, most of my co-workers, almost all of my modest number of lovers—were white.

Many people have the recurring dream about being in college and taking a final exam for which they are not the least bit prepared. My dream has always been a little different: I'm enrolled in a class that I've barely attended; I don't know when the final is, what assignments are due, or what my standing in the class is, but I realize, with rising dread and guilt, that it can't be good. From time to time, in my waking life, I had a similar feeling about the way I was living. I hadn't paid enough attention—whatever that might mean—to being black; that had consequences, surely, never mind that I didn't know what they were.

I couldn't easily have said why I felt that way. You could say, in fact, that I was living the way I'd been taught. I did not grow up in a family whose members came home every night talking about what the hated Whitey had done to them that day. I learned from my family to accept others, from the boys in Lincoln Heights to the friend Wanda brought home from college once when I was in kindergarten, the first white person I remember crossing our doorway—a guitar-playing young woman with long blond hair who laughed at *Gilligan's Island* with me. What was wrong, then? What was wrong was that I lived in America, where being without a clear racial designation was like being in junior high school without a homeroom. And it wasn't enough to simply *be* black, or white, or Asian, or Hispanic, or Native American, or Jewish, or whatever: you had to act the part, or you got talked about, if not worse. ("You *know* he went out with somebody *white* last year." "She dates *black* men.") During my time at Doubleday there was one other black assistant, a woman my age. Ever meet a member of the opposite sex whom you like but don't feel compelled to ask out, for whatever reason? That was how I felt about this woman. (And not because she was too dark for me.) But since she was black and I was black, our colleagues acted as if it was our duty to get married. Marshall said so once, in almost those words; one of my other fellow assistants, a white guy, made a comment implying that I had committed a kind of sin of omission.

I quote *Dreams from My Father*, by Barack Obama: "That was the problem with people like Joyce. They talked about the richness of their multicultural heritage and it sounded real good, until you noticed that they avoided black people." Perhaps, Mr. President, that's because liberal whites—whatever prejudices they may harbor inside—are generally the ones who at least pay lip service, in our post–civil rights society, to the idea of race's unimportance. (They did so around me, anyway; never having been to an all-white gathering, I of course cannot vouch for what happens at them. Yes, yes, I know—they could be talking about me and blacks in general like dogs. Nothing they could say, though, would be worse than what I know for a fact some blacks have said about me out of my earshot. Yes, yes—at least in that situation it's my own people talking about me. If you want to think that makes it better, go ahead.) It's true that I hung out with white people because, in college and at work, that was mostly who I met—just as I had met mostly black folks in DC. It's also true, I have to admit, that I worried that blacks I met would disapprove of my life and history. This is not to say that black people had a monopoly on disapproval. I remember the reactions of a couple of whites when they heard about my dating history. Their faces contorted as they struggled against their temptation to ask me to explain myself, to say exactly what it was I had against black women, anyway. Some won the struggle; others did not. What I found more unsettling, though, were the reactions of some well-meaning blacks. Occasionally, when I was around a group of blacks, one of them would make some casual remark that disparaged whites, and another would whisper in the ear of the speaker—whereupon the speaker would say something to the effect of "Oops, I forgot," having obviously been reminded that I was dating, or had dated, somebody white.

I don't want to give the impression that I dropped from Neptune at age twenty-five and couldn't understand blacks' antipathy toward whites. I'd had my run-ins with good old-fashioned white racism, as comparatively minor as they may seem. Some of it was the annoying everyday variety. I had been followed out of stores; I had shown up at a job site at nine a.m. on the day an ad appeared in the paper, only to be told that the job had been "filled"; once, during my freshman year of college, as I sat in the library with my copy of *Jane Eyre*, a young white woman I didn't know asked me, "Why are you reading that?" (I kicked myself afterward for not giving her a lecture, but in retrospect I think my response was the right one: "It's for my English class.") Going up from there, we have the time I went to look at an apartment in Windsor Terrace, Brooklyn, and was told by the man showing it, "I feel like shit saying this, but if I'd known you were black I never would've told you to come. The neighbors wouldn't let you live here." A year after that, I went to Boston on Doubleday's dime to attend the publication party for a book by Mary Helen Washington, which Gerald had edited. I stayed with my Oberlin-in-London pal (and now novelist) David Maine and his then-girlfriend; while I was there we had a visit from our London-semester pals Mark Sanders, Jena Osman, and Kate Davis, who had driven from Brown University. After those three left for the drive back to Brown, the hippie-looking Dave, who lived to make jokes, had the bright idea of running to a nearby alley, at the point where Mark and the others would turn onto a major street, and heading them off at the pass. As we were booking down the sidewalk, I became aware of a car speeding backwards parallel to us; when it beat us to the alley, two white cops jumped out, gripping the pistols in their holsters, one of them shouting, "Awright, get your fuckin' hands in the air!" Dave and I, not wanting to die that day, did exactly as we were told, then were informed that we'd begun running near a store that had been held up recently. Ah, of course; *that* was why they'd chased us down like escaped convicts and made ready to pump bullets into us. A simple mistake, that was all.

Most painfully—because of how unutterably stupid I felt afterward—there was one day in the summer of 1983, when I was between my sophomore and junior years of college and looking for work. After answering a newspaper ad announcing openings for salespeople, I left 232 in my best suit and trekked to a town in suburban Maryland—or maybe it was Virginia—where I discovered that, rather than an interview, I had come to a group orientation. Ten or twelve of us, all dressed as if for church, sat at a rectangular table and listened as a trim, dark-haired, smooth-voiced man of perhaps early middle age gave us the low-down on selling Cutco knives. When the man had finished his talk, which was sprinkled liberally with witty asides and self-deprecating humor, he passed out applications for us to fill out. I was about half-done with mine when the man summoned me into a separate room. In a pleasant tone, he asked me questions based on the part of the application I'd completed; beyond that, for better or worse, my memory of the incident becomes a tad fuzzy. All I know is that the man spoke words of such an innocuous, inoffensive nature that I not only had trouble remembering them later but failed to question what lay behind them at the time. Not until after I'd left that office without completing my application was I struck by the one conceivable reason why I had been led to do so: of the dozen or so people seated at the rectangular table, only I was black.

As angry as those experiences made me, they didn't cause me to hate all white people; the whites who were my friends were as angry about those episodes as I was. I believed, as I had always believed, in judging people individually. But just as an umbrella won't keep you one hundred percent dry in a rainstorm, a belief in treating everyone as an individual will not keep you from absorbing the prevailing ideas in a nation that is, when it comes to race, neurotic if not plain crazy. In an unreasonable world, the reasonable man comes to feel he is doing something wrong.

I was not so deluded or so lacking in pride and self-esteem that I considered myself white, and—this is important—I didn't *want* to be white. But if black people felt unable to talk freely in front of me ("Oops, I forgot"), then, some part of me asked, could I really be black? And if I wasn't, in this nation where you had to be *something*, then what was I?

At a party in Brooklyn one spring night in 1988, a group of us editorial assistants were standing in a circle; it was very late, we had all been drinking, and we were having the kind of frank discussion produced by such conditions. The discussion must have had something to do with the pros and cons of asserting one's cultural identity. The host was the same fellow who took me to task for not dating the black assistant; I'll call him Mark, since, actually, that was his name. "That's one of the reasons I like Cliff so much," Mark said to the others about me at one point. "It's not because he talks like a white guy, it's because he isn't *anything*."

===

In late May of that year, in one of the periodic bloodlettings at Doubleday, Marshall was fired. That left me in rather the same position as the chicken's body I'd seen Uncle Manson separate from its head years earlier. (When Jackie Onassis heard the news, she walked over to my desk with a stricken look on her face and kissed me on the forehead. My Oberlin friend Charles Hawley, hearing that story, said in outrage, "That's what you'd do to a child!" Could be. But how many people do you know who were kissed by Jacqueline Kennedy Onassis?) I soon met with Herman Gollob, the company's fiftyish, short, white-haired, gutter-mouthed editor in chief. Herman was later to write a book about his late-blooming passion for Shakespeare, but the Bard didn't appear to be speaking through him when he talked to me. He said that he would like to do something for me—i.e., promote me to editor—but that I was "attached to Marshall like a fuckin' umbilical cord." That did my ego no good but was probably just as well, given how I'd come to feel about book publishing; still, it raised the question of what I would do for things like food and rent.

Then several things happened at once. Marshall's replacement, a very pleasant woman brought in from outside, offered to keep me on as her assistant; a woman at *Family Circle* magazine, the identical twin sister of a Doubleday editor, offered me a job at $19,000 a year—no fortune even then, but more than I'd made at Doubleday; and the editor Loretta's terrorized former assistant (the one who had kept typing "Executive Idiot") left her current job and asked if I was interested in replacing her. This was a straight word-processing/data-entry gig at the World Financial Center office of American Express, specifically Amex's philanthropic foundation.

It was a boring, dead-end job, but it was part-time—no more than three days a week, Monday through Wednesday—and paid what seemed to me the princely sum of $17.50 per hour. What this meant was that I could earn pretty much what I'd made at Doubleday, but spend every Thursday and Friday writing! I took the job. Wednesday became the new Friday. I put my severance pay from Doubleday toward my first home computer, and armed with that gleaming machine, I set out to slay two dragons: the novel and the subject of race.

There was the tradition, in the works I had loved, of the confused boy/man against the world: Charlie Brown dealing with the cruelty and thoughtlessness of other children, who were stand-ins for the unfairness of life; Spider-Man's alter-ego, Peter Parker, fighting villains in his costume and loneliness out of it; Holden Caulfield struggling against phoniness and his own psychological problems; Ben Braddock in *The Graduate* rejecting the bourgeois world's expectations of him. I took a stab at continuing the lineage with my main character, a twenty-three-year-old, black New Yorker and professional comic-book illustrator named Adam James, who straddled the worlds of blacks and whites.

I made an interesting discovery that summer about writing, or, rather, about people's attitudes about writing. When I mentioned that I worked in an office two-and-a-half-to-three days a week and spent the rest of my time at home working on fiction, many thought—well, I don't know for sure, since no one ever said anything directly, but as far as I could tell it was either that (1) spending one's days writing fiction, for someone who obviously wasn't Stephen King and didn't even have a book contract, was a silly thing to be doing, or (2) "writing" actually meant eating Ben & Jerry's ice cream out of the carton in front of *Odd Couple* reruns. A good friend of mine asked me one day—a question that brought him a piece of my mind—"On your days off, do you *just write*?" I told some guy at a party that I spent Thursday, Friday, and often either Saturday or Sunday writing, and that I got started around 8:30 a.m.; clearly not knowing what to make of that, he stared at a point beyond my shoulder and said after a moment, his voice trailing off, "By 8:30, so much has already been done . . ." Still others, unable to comprehend my days "off," focused instead on my job at American Express, and since *that* wasn't far beyond the capability of a trained monkey, they didn't get what I was doing with my life.

I shouldn't complain, since, with my new arrangement, I had one hell of a good time. And that's why no one should have doubted that I was actually writing during my days at home: for me, nothing is more fun. That isn't to say that writing is not a struggle and a challenge—it's both—but that's where the fun is, and that applies to both fiction and nonfiction. I have heard some aspiring novelists say that they find the writing process to be torture, which—given the steep odds against finding a publisher, the equally steep odds against having your miraculously published work catch on with a significant portion of the public, and the humbling, staggering, brain-overloading numbers of people doing exactly what you're doing—always makes me want to ask: Why do it?

That summer Marie Brown, the agent I'd met through Gerald, told me about an open call for submissions for an anthology of African-American fiction to be published by Penguin Books. The outside editor for the book, whom I'd never heard of, had published one novel and had a second about to come out; her name was Terry McMillan. I put my novel about Adam James aside for a bit and wrote a twenty-five-page, semi-autobiographical story. Titled "Circle," it moved back and forth between a black boy's experiences with his family in his hometown of Washington, DC, and events years later, on a college campus, where the same boy (whom I named after my brother) dates a black young woman and then a white one. I showed the story to Gerald, who was outraged over the interracial parts—specifically, that the main character ends up with the white woman. He told me, "I read it and thought, '*This* is what he wants to publish?'" He interpreted the story (and he wasn't alone, as it turned out) as a comment on black women; intending no such thing, I saw it as a story about, among other issues, the breaking of an idiotic taboo. Without changing a word, I mailed the story off, then forgot about it.

Meanwhile, that summer of '88, a new face appeared on my personal Mount Rushmore of creative heroes. Charles M. Schulz, Muhammad Ali, Stan Lee, J. D. Salinger, and Bill Cosby made room for James Baldwin. Dusting off the books Gerald had given me, I started with *Go Tell It on the Mountain*, which I enjoyed, but the novel that made a convert out of me—and that was, ironically, as I was to discover later, one of Baldwin's most critically reviled works—was *Tell Me How Long the Train's Been Gone*, with its portrait of an interracial couple. I read *Another Country* and *Giovanni's*

Room, then moved on to the nonfiction with *Nobody Knows My Name, No Name in the Street, The Fire Next Time*, and *Notes of a Native Son*. By that time I had read Ralph Ellison's *Invisible Man* and was familiar with the work of Charles Chesnutt, Richard Wright, Toni Morrison, Alice Walker, Gloria Naylor, John Edgar Wideman, and other black writers, but I encountered in Baldwin what I hadn't known existed: one who condemned white racism in no uncertain terms but also questioned blacks' indiscriminate hatred of whites. I felt as if I had spent years in an integrated lunatic asylum and finally found the one other sane person there. Baldwin wrote in *The Fire Next Time* about meeting with Elijah Muhammad of the Nation of Islam, "I knew two or three people, white, whom I would trust with my life, and I knew a few others, white, who were struggling as hard as they knew how, and with great effort and sweat and risk, to make the world more human. But how could I say this?" But it wasn't Baldwin's views on race alone that appealed to me. I was enchanted by the music of those epic sentences; and I felt that Baldwin's voice, in all its wisdom, exasperation, and humanity, was speaking directly to me.

Tell Me How Long the Train's Been Gone and Another Country were published, and at least partly set, during the decade that produced me—but of which I had few memories; reading those novels, I felt I was experiencing my own private 1960s. When I think of that hot, hot summer of '88, and picture myself hanging out with friends or shirtless on my fire escape trying to cool off, my memories are tinged with evocations of the '60s from Baldwin's books—that magical-seeming decade, in all of its idealism, struggle, and hope, in its belief that we really could all be one people.

My excitement about Baldwin moved Gerald to re-read the books, whose content he had largely forgotten. He was as disapproving of the interracial romance in *Tell Me How Long the Train's Been Gone* as he had been of the one in my short story. We argued over that and many other things race-related, arguments that were usually friendly and usually won by him. We had a number of these debates on our way to or from the movies we saw together (including the wonderful *The Gods Must Be Crazy II* and the searing *A Dry White Season*). Gerald would walk along leisurely, in the long black raincoat he often wore, idly singing lines from gospel songs during lulls in our conversation—he had once, he told me, traveled with a choir. While he sang next to me I tried to think of ways around his logic. I remember, once, attacking what I saw as the insanity of the taboos against crossing racial lines and the guilt internalized, for no reason, even by those who did it. Amused, Gerald referred to a former Doubleday colleague of ours, a white woman we'll call Debbie. He was, somewhat incongruously, friendly with Debbie, who was a couple of years older than me and had had a position far above mine; more pertinently here, she may or may not have been romantically interested in me, because I could never tell how serious she was when she talked about it. "So," Gerald said, "you want to be able to fuck Debbie and not feel guilty about it."

"*No!*" I said, only partly feigning frustration, before adding, "*Yeah!*"
Gerald went into one of his belly laughs.

===

Baldwin, who was born in 1924 (the same year as Ma), was raised in Harlem, the scene of most of his novels. A few months after I began reading them, when I decided I'd had enough of the treks to and from the apartment where I lived waaaaay out in Brooklyn, Gerald—my advocate in all things—told me about an apartment he knew of, in Harlem. It was above his mother's place. She lived in one of three funky little green houses on 150th Street that had been divided into apartments, one per floor; the landlady, an older woman named Mrs. Johnson, lived in one too. In April 1989 I became Mrs. Johnson's tenant and the upstairs neighbor of Gerald's mother, Mrs. Gladney, who was as sweet and kind as her son was caustic. Together, those two ladies saw every move I made. Gerald told me that he said to himself, "What have I gotten this boy into"; that was after a phone call from his mother, who reported that I had turned right and then left after leaving home, and so was probably going to see the agent Marie Brown on 154th Street. Another time, Gerald told me that his mother had told him that Mrs. Johnson had told *her* that a young white woman had visited me. (And here we see in action the absurdity of American attitudes about race: the black Mrs. Johnson was *at least* as light-skinned as my visitor.) About the only event both ladies missed was the night, late in 1990, when someone came in through my bedroom window and emptied the apartment of everything but the floorboards.

Chester Himes wrote about an event almost identical to that one in *The Big Gold Dream*, one of his priceless Harlem novels featuring the black police detectives Grave Digger Jones and Coffin Ed Johnson. In another, *The Crazy Kill,* Grave Digger tells another character that in Harlem, "folks . . . do things for reasons nobody else in the world would think of. Listen, there were two hard working colored jokers, both with families, got to fighting in a bar . . . and cut each other to death over whether Paris was in France or France was in Paris." Ralph Ellison picked up that theme in "Harlem Is Nowhere," an essay in his terrific collection *Shadow and Act*: "The most surreal fantasies are acted out upon the streets of Harlem; a man ducks in and out of traffic shouting and throwing imaginary grenades that actually exploded during World War I; a boy participates in the rape-robbery of his mother; a man beating his wife in a park uses boxing 'science' and observes Marquess of Queensbury rules . . . ; two men hold a third while a lesbian slashes him to death with a razor blade; boy gangsters wielding homemade pistols . . . shoot down their young rivals. Life becomes a masquerade, exotic costumes are worn every day. Those who cannot afford to hire a horse wear riding habits; others who could not afford a hunting trip or who seldom attend sporting events carry shooting sticks."

I never saw anything as crazy as that in Harlem, though I didn't have to search long, or, really, at all, for extra-legal activities—customer-hunters walking around saying "Smoke?" and "Sssssssex." And from time to time I wondered if what I saw was actually there. Once I passed an immaculately dressed man, in a brown pinstriped suit, shiny leather shoes, and tie—lying on his back in front of the door of a bodega. The owner, stepping over the man to get outside, half-shouted at and half-pleaded with him to get up, whereupon the man reached into a jacket pocket, pulled out a cigarette, and quietly asked for a light. Then there was the occasional sight of a young woman, who lived in the house behind mine, going down my fire escape— having escaped through her window and across my roof from a fight with her boyfriend, of which I could hear every word.

Most of the people I met in Harlem, though, were like the ones Baldwin had written about: ordinary folks trying to get by. In the little green house adjacent to mine lived an older man, Raymon Hartso, who was about as friendly as he could be and reminded me of my uncles; I have fond memories of shooting the breeze with Raymon while I was on my stoop and he was on his, feeling a little like I was back on Division Avenue. But I spent most of my time in my bedroom in front of my computer, writing, sipping rum-laced coffee, while, on my turntable, jazz records played.

Continuing my tradition of movies leading me to music—*Cooley High* to Motown, *The Graduate* to Simon & Garfunkel, *A Charlie Brown Christmas* to Vince Guaraldi—in the fall of 1988 I had seen Clint Eastwood's film *Bird*. "Bird," of course, was the nickname of the groundbreaking jazz alto saxophonist Charlie Parker (1920–55), played masterfully in the film by Forest Whitaker. I can't swear that I knew who Parker was before seeing *Bird*, but afterward I bought the movie soundtrack. I didn't understand then that sound engineers had transplanted Bird's solos from his recordings of the 1940s and '50s into new studio sessions. I was later to read Stanley Crouch's opinion that that approach had robbed the record of the organic feel that results when musicians play together and build on one another's ideas. For me, though, the effect was to isolate Bird's sound. What a sound: as bright and fast as a light beam, as thin and hard as the needles Parker jabbed into his veins, and able to evoke anything, from complex ideas to the most basic heartfelt emotions. Branching out from Bird, I checked out Blue Note collections of jazz tunes by Thelonious Monk (*Genius of Modern Music, Volume 1*) and Sonny Rollins (*Volume 1*). In the personal crisis that was headed my way in the next few years, this music was to be an invaluable ally.

In the meantime, I had, or so it seemed to me, finished my novel *The Ballad of Adam James*. Adam, in retrospect, hadn't arrived at any stunning conclusions about race, which is not surprising, given that his creator hadn't, either. Gerald read it, saying that he found a big part of it "plotless" but that he "laughed all the way through." I sent the manuscript to Marie Brown, who made occasional noises about submitting it to publishers but showed very few signs of doing it.

Then, one day in the summer of 1989, I was doing my monkey work at American Express when Marie called. Terry McMillan, she said, had accepted my story for her anthology of black fiction. Soon Terry herself—whose novel *Waiting to Exhale* was to make her a superstar a couple of years later—called me. She told me I was a "good writer" and that she wanted my story because of its interracial theme, which hadn't come up in the other submissions; she also said that she wanted the story to focus more on that theme, as much as she liked the parts about the main character's family. I liked the family parts, too, but I loved the idea of breaking into print, of having something to show for the way I was living. I said okay. I didn't feel tortured about it; for a while, in fact, I walked about two feet above the ground.

While I waited for the anthology to come out, I devoted the summer of 1990 to writing short stories, several of which later appeared in "literary journals that nobody read, including me," as the narrator of a Tobias Wolff story, a young aspiring writer, put it. It took a while for even that to happen, and in the meantime the rejection letters rolled in like the tide. As much as I liked my writing life, there were moments when, if I didn't succumb to despair, I could sense it on my trail. My story in Terry McMillan's anthology was to come out in a few months, but sometimes that one triumph seemed like a lone star, pointing up the cloudiness of the rest of the sky. Was I really going to succeed at this? And if I wasn't, then what was I—a twenty-seven-year-old part-time word processor—going to succeed at? Where, exactly, had that sense of my own specialness, left over from my junior-high days, led me? Had my teachers in DC sold me, had I sold myself, a bill of goods?

Breaking Ice, the anthology, appeared at the end of that summer. Its fifty-seven stories and novel excerpts included pieces by Amiri Baraka, Rita Dove, Ernest Gaines, Charles Johnson, James Alan McPherson, Gloria Naylor, Alice Walker, John Edgar Wideman . . . and me. Joyce Carol Oates's review of the book in the *Washington Post* mentioned my story, now called "Judgment," by name; the review in the *Chicago Tribune* concluded with a few lines from it. Around the time that the book was published, Amy, my girlfriend, told me that she and I had been invited to a Sunday-afternoon cocktail party at the Park Slope, Brooklyn, apartment of a couple she knew. I walked into the apartment to the sound of applause, and among the smiling faces I saw was my old DC pal Kev. It was a party to celebrate my story in *Breaking Ice*; Amy had arranged the whole thing.

On the flip side, Gerald made a point of telling me that his teenage son, Kamau, had shown "Judgment" to some of his friends, who were black. "They hate you," Gerald said.

Interlude

On a Sunday in the late summer of 1989, I saw that *Lawrence of Arabia* was playing downtown that evening. (When you live on 150th Street, most of Manhattan is downtown.) After calling around on extremely short notice in search of company for that nearly four-hour movie, I saw it with my old London-semester comrade Jena Osman. I tried Jena in part because earlier, and very much out of the blue, I had called my pal Charles Hawley's former girlfriend Amy Peck, who had said—in a not-uncharacteristic reply, I was to find—"Are you crazy?" Whether or not Amy thought I was crazy, I entered her mind, she told me later, as someone to possibly see movies with. That was why, a while afterward, the two of us went to a theater in Greenwich Village to check out a very odd film called *The Navigator.* When it was over, Amy, as she told me later, assumed we were going our separate ways; I assumed we were eating together. We ate together. Over dinner at Pizzeria Uno on Sixth Avenue, Amy—as she told me later—was surprised to find herself comfortable enough to talk about her family and recall collecting acorns with her two younger siblings in Washington, DC, in their grandmother's yard.

We did more things together, I and this slender woman with the short blond hair and unusually, intriguingly wide eyes. We went to a concert in Prospect Park, in my old stomping grounds of Park Slope, where she lived; we went to a downtown bar for an Oberlin-organized fundraiser on behalf of David Dinkins, who was soon to be New York's first black mayor. We must have talked about publishing; Amy was an assistant editor at Farrar, Straus & Giroux, where her mother (dead for a decade by then) had met her father (who had died the year before mine). One day I mentioned to another friend that I'd had a good time recently with Amy, and I added, realizing it as I spoke, "I always have a good time with her." I had discovered that beneath Amy's sometimes startling directness ("Are you crazy?") was real warmth; the first time she touched me in a meaningful way, putting her hand on my forearm as we sat in a restaurant, was after I told her how I worried about my grandmother.

In 1989 autumn arrived on Saturday, September 23, at around one p.m.; I know that because Amy and I, she in a sleeveless yellow top, were crossing a street in the Village, on our way to see *Dr. Strangelove*, when we felt the temperature fall. There was a lot of falling that day.

The Spanish Tinge

James Baldwin's voice was one I could follow anywhere. I happily read his writing on subjects I wouldn't have investigated, at least not then, on my own: Norman Mailer, whose books I hadn't yet read, or Ingmar Bergman, whose films I hadn't yet seen. Little wonder, then, that I have gone back numerous times to his essay "The Discovery of What It Means to Be an American," which is about race and being a writer. That essay's impact on me was strongest when I was in my mid-twenties, but, partly for that reason, I now understand the impact in a way I didn't, at least not fully or consciously, at the time. What I find clearer today are both the differences and the similarities between the situation Baldwin found himself in as a young man and the one I was struggling with. This sentence from his essay provides vivid examples of both: "I was as isolated from Negroes as I was from whites, which is what happens when a Negro begins, at bottom, to believe what white people say about him." What (some) white people say, of course, is that blacks are inferior, if not worthless; therefore, just as Baldwin was isolated for obvious reasons from whites, he felt apart from blacks because on some level he believed in their inferiority and did not want to be identified with it. A symptom: "I had never listened to Bessie Smith . . . in the same way that, for years, I would not touch watermelon."

Here is the sentence I might have written: "I was isolated from black people, which is what happens when a black person begins, at bottom, to believe what some blacks say about him." To put the differences between Baldwin's predicament and mine in the simplest possible terms: Baldwin had internalized the message that he was not white enough, and I had internalized the message that I was not black enough. I had grown up listening to recordings of the "I Have a Dream" speech, hearing the slogan "Black is beautiful," watching critically acclaimed TV shows about black families, playing with G.I. Joes that had kinky hair, seeing people wear dashikis—in short, seeing signs that blackness was a well-regarded thing in the world; and while that came with baggage I could have done without, it protected me, as I now see, from hating myself because I wasn't white. Baldwin had no such protection, and I give him credit: he pulled himself out of a hole that probably would have been too deep for me.

He pulled himself out as a result of going to Europe. "I left America," he wrote in the essay, "because I doubted my ability to survive the fury of the color problem here. . . . I wanted to prevent myself from becoming *merely* a Negro; or, even, merely a Negro writer. I wanted to find out in what way the *specialness* of my experience could be made to connect me with other people instead of dividing me from them. . . . In my necessity to find the terms on which my experience could be related to others, Negroes and whites, writers and non-writers, I proved, to my astonishment, to be as American as any Texas G.I." (italics Baldwin's). He wrote about the white American writers he met in France, "The fact that I was the son of a slave and they were the sons of free men meant less, by the time we confronted each other on European soil, than the fact that we were both searching for our separate identities. When we had found these, we seemed to be saying, why, then, we would no longer need to cling to the shame and bitterness which had divided us so long. It became terribly clear in Europe . . . that, no matter where our fathers had been born, or what they had endured, the fact of Europe had formed us both, was part of our identity and part of our inheritance." The discovery of that "inheritance" evidently caused him to see a need for something else, too, because he soon "suffered a species of breakdown" that necessitated going to "the mountains of Switzerland . . . armed with two Bessie Smith records and a typewriter." There, he wrote, "I began to try to re-create the life that I had first known as a child and from which I had spent so many years in flight. It was Bessie Smith, through her tone and her cadence, who helped me to dig back to the way I myself must have spoken when I was a pickaninny, and to remember the things I had heard and seen and felt. . . . She helped to reconcile me to being a 'nigger.'"

My own problem wasn't that I was unreconciled to being a "nigger"; I understood, accepted, and—contrary to what some must have thought— was proud of the fact that I was black. But I could certainly relate to the need to "find out in what way . . . my experience could be made to connect me with other people instead of dividing me from them." Since Baldwin had found what he sought in Europe . . .

Over breakfast in a Park Slope diner one Saturday morning in May of 1990, when I had been dating Amy for about eight months, I told her something I'd been mulling over. As she listened she told herself not to get upset; I was thinking out loud about possible future plans, that was all. When she realized that what I'd been thinking about included her, the conversation took on new life. By the time we left the diner, our minds were made up, our plan hatched. Amy, who had asked if I was crazy when I called at the last minute about going to the movies, agreed on the spot to spend a year or so with me in Spain.

Unlike in England, where I was in Oberlin's good hands, this would be an adventure of the self; I would make it, or not, on my own. To the inevitable question "Why Spain?," the answer boiled down to, "Why *not* Spain?" Amy and I had both spent time in England already, and although we had no particular ties to other European countries, I'd always liked the sound of the word "Spain." I started saving money for the trip, each week putting forty dollars in cash in the pages of a big book of Baldwin's nonfiction, called, appropriately enough, *The Price of the Ticket*.

Shortly after my apartment in Harlem was burgled, I rented a moving truck, loaded what was left of my stuff into it while Gerald's mother stood crying on the porch, said my goodbyes, and drove that sucker to Amy's studio apartment in Park Slope. Around that same time, tired of waiting for Marie Brown to sell my novel, I sent it to another agent, Faith Childs, who had me revise the book and then agreed to send it around. Then Amy and I put our belongings in storage. On January 4, 1991 we flew to that city of wonderfully weird buildings, siestas, motorscooters, beer with breakfast, 10-p.m. dinners, dirt-cheap wine, and unrepentant smokers: Barcelona.

The wonder of our trip, when I think back on it, is that no one told us we were insane—unless that's what people meant when they said "brave."

Amy and I arrived at midnight at the Pension L'Isard, in south-central Barcelona, greeted by the very understanding couple who ran that squat, boxlike, not at all beautiful place not far from the Mediterranean. We had an open reservation for a second-floor room there; we had our luggage, a few hundred dollars in travelers' checks, and, in terms of what was needed to live for a year, almost nothing else. We had no permanent place to live and no leads for finding one; ditto for jobs; we didn't even speak Spanish. In the fall we had both taken a Spanish class at the New School, back in New York, but we were far, very far, from fluency, and to make matters more challenging, people in Barcelona spoke not Spanish but Catalan, a sort of like-minded first cousin of Spanish, one that was very fond of x's. Our plan was to get very busy, very quickly, in finding work and an apartment, and to pick up the language as we went. Every morning we woke as early as we could—which for the first week or so was not very early—to buy a news-paper and look at apartment ads. Then, in those days before cell phones, we would use the payphone in the bar down the street from the *pension*, making for a daily Spanish-language version of the old Abbott & Costello "Who's on First?" routine. During the calls in which we could actually com-municate, we learned that realtors wanted anywhere from two to eleven months' rent up front, which was out of the question for us. Not feeling dis-couraged enough, we would next walk around Barcelona looking for jobs, finding a surprising number of people who spoke just enough English to tell us politely to get lost. And then there was the eating problem. Our room had no refrigerator; if we wanted to buy groceries to avoid burning through all of our money in restaurants, we were limited to food that wouldn't go bad at room temperature, which made for some dubious meals. (Not that our room was warm. Winter in Barcelona was like winter in London: you were never cold outside and never warm inside.) We were so budget-minded that it was only after days of smelling roasted sweet potatoes, sold by a woman with a stand on the corner, that we broke down and bought some.

"I feel like we're in Dickens's London," I said to Amy as we stood there munching.

"If we were," she said, "at least we'd speak the language."

Every day seemed to bring frustration, which after a couple of weeks verged on despair. The mood crystallized one evening as we drank beer in a dimly lit bar near the *pension*. We felt too grim to talk much, which was just as well, since anything we said would've amounted to a single question: What have we done?

Somehow, those bleak days seemed to me a good time to start my second novel, *Fat Jammin' Joe and the Simple City Cats*, about a DC-born jazz pianist and his three Lincoln Heights musician friends. For an hour or so each evening, I would sit at a small wooden table in a bar carpeted with cigarette butts, nursing a decent, dirt-cheap (30- peseta) glass of red wine and scribbling in my marble composition book. When I got back to the *pension,* Amy would fan the air with her hand to drive away the smell of smoke.

And then things started to get better—though not before a ridiculous episode.

We went to the American Express office on Passeig de Gracia every couple of days or so to cash travelers' checks and pick up our at-first-nonexistent mail. The people in the office were nice, and our dealings with them were pleasantly innocuous. Then, one day, we walked in to find men armed with Uzis, one of whom restrained—with difficulty—a loudly snarling German shepherd that would otherwise have had us for lunch. We were frightened and mystified, and then we understood: the Persian Gulf War had just begun. I remembered the graffiti I'd seen around Barcelona, reading *Guerra no!* ("No war!"). Symbols of the United States, such as the American Express office, were now considered targets.

Meanwhile: in our growing desperation to find an apartment, we had put up signs around the city. In what felt like a miracle, we got a call at the *pension* from a woman with an affordable room. As Amy and I were on our way to see her, I was nagged by an idea. To prove to myself that it was silly and drive it from my mind, I mentioned it to Amy. Imagine reaching for a fire extinguisher and discovering too late that it's a can of gasoline. By the time we got to the apartment, we had half-convinced ourselves that the signs we'd put up—which described us as young Americans—had been seen by anti-war terrorist kidnappers, whom we were now going to meet. How else to explain our sudden good luck, this milk from a stone? The apartment building was separated by a very narrow street from an outdoor odds-and-ends market; for quite a while, Amy and I stood in front of the market, hands in the pockets of our jackets, unable to pass up the apartment yet afraid we'd never be seen again if we went inside. Every so often a young, dark-haired woman appeared on a second-floor balcony of the building across the street, looking more annoyed each time. Finally, she came out the front door and walked up to us, asking in accented English if we were the people she had talked to about the room. Finally able to see our fears for what they were, as embarrassed as we'd ever been in our lives, we said yes. Clearly angry, the woman said that she now didn't have time to show us the room but that we could call her later.

Everyone was in a better mood the day we saw the apartment, which we took. To celebrate, Amy and I treated ourselves in a restaurant on Balmes, a creperie we returned to often. There, we made a friend, the waiter José, a cherubic, mustached, ever-smiling sweetheart of a man who, with his back straight and head held high, was *maybe* four foot nine. José's English was even worse than our Spanish, which is to say he spoke none. For that reason our communication was all in Spanish, and we felt pride that we were able to tell him things—pride that turned to horror when our language skills improved and we realized what we'd said. "I want to I work," I told the patiently smiling José, while Amy pointed at me and informed our friend, "He is to write." When we'd ask for the check, José would first bring us free glasses of liqueur.

It was now early February. Around that time we also made headway on the job front. Amy got babysitting gigs and freelance editing work from the States, and I was taken on by a language school, Langage Idiomas, run by a tall, balding, funny American named David Donaldson, who sent me to various companies to give executives English lessons; I also had one private student. Finally, I got a check for $500—enough to set up a Spanish bank account—for a short story I'd sold in the States. As we lugged our belongings via Metro to our new apartment, Amy said, "It's the end of the beginning."

Simona, the non-terrorist young woman with the room for rent, lived a ways north of the *pension*, in Gracia, a neighborhood in central Barcelona with a bohemian feel and the narrowest streets and sidewalks I'd ever seen. As for the apartment, you might get something similar if you crossed the U.N. with Grand Central Station. Ours wasn't the only room Simona rented out. A lot of young people, mostly men, stayed there on the way to and from seemingly every place on the planet; our room had a curtain instead of a door, the better to hear the opera and heavy-metal records, guitar playing, and loud conversations that went on much of the day and night in many languages, none of which—fortunately—we could understand. The temperature in the apartment was no higher than in the *pension*, but Simona kindly lent us a heater for which we bought cans of gas. The thing I remember best about that room was the wooden table that had been stained orange and turned everything that came into contact with it the same color. That, and the shower down the hall, one that gave you the choice of washing the whole room or using a shower curtain that wrapped around you like a vertical sleeping bag. The saving grace of the place, even more welcome than the heater, was the kitchen. We could cook, and, since there was money coming in, we could buy and store food, including cardboard cartons of pretty decent red wine.

We were almost comfortable, which gave us the chance to do what we hadn't before: observe and enjoy Barcelona. The city is built on a gentle slope that runs down to the Mediterranean. At the top of it is Tibidabo, a mountain complete with an amusement park; looking south from its peak, you feel you can hold all of Barcelona in your hand, like a snow globe. For the opposite sensation—the feeling of being a small creature in an alien landscape without end—you can head southeast to Parc Guell, the work of Gaudi, whose curves, animal sculptures, winding paths, and multicolored tiles bring to mind New York's Central Park as designed by Dr. Seuss. Gaudi is best-known for the façade to the Sagrada Familia, but his work can also be seen on wavy buildings—resembling stills from a hallucination—on the Ramblas, the beautiful tree-lined strip with its shops, cafes, and outdoor sellers of flowers and birds. Soon we discovered Sitges, a beach town just outside Barcelona, reachable by commuter train. It was there, sitting next to Amy at a small outdoor table in the cool air, leather jacket on, drinking a beer, looking out at the blue-green water, that I first felt truly glad I had come to Spain.

Amy and I took in Barcelona mainly on foot, while the Spaniards took us in, sometimes with open stares—directed for the most part, of course, at me. The stares were different from the hostile looks from white Americans when a black man wanders into the wrong bar; there was an innocence about them, a simple wonder and curiosity at something rarely seen.

One afternoon, going to the apartment of Alfonso, my private student, whom I had taught for several months, I took along a cassette player and a tape of Sam Cooke songs. I played "Bring It on Home" for him, and we discussed the lyrics. Then Alfonso left the room, returning with an LP of American soul hits. My smile faltered when I saw the image on the front cover: an egg decorated to look like a black person, or, more accurately, like somebody's idea of one, with ink-black skin and ridiculously big red lips. A certain amount of affection had developed between Alfonso and me over the months; I knew that he meant well and that he had no inkling of why a black person might be offended by the image, and I didn't have the heart to tell him. My attitude was a bit different the day Amy and I were in a store and I saw a plastic bag of chocolate candy, the logo a caricature of an African child—spear in hand, barely dressed, black as midnight except for monstrously huge eyes and lips like two inflated red rafts. I popped as many of those candies between thumb and forefinger as I could before Amy stopped me, not because she was unsympathetic but because she didn't want me to end up in a Spanish jail over a bag of chocolates.

And there, it seemed to me, you had the difference between Spain and the United States, racially speaking: innocence, with all its charm, guilelessness, good intentions, and pitfalls, versus experience, its wheels greased with cynicism. A white American store owner might hate me, but he knows what would happen to his store if he stocked candy decorated with jungle bunnies. (Exceptions are stores I've entered in the South, where it's a different ball game.) Spain might seem to have the upper hand here, but then, where in Spain could I sit on a stoop and shoot the breeze with a Raymon Hartso, who has certain experiences in common with me just by virtue of his skin color? You decide what you can live with.

I kept writing. Barcelona has what looks at first glance like the world's biggest garbage dump but turns out, on closer inspection, to be a peerlessly grand flea market. There, a man wearing a wool cap, glasses, and several sweaters haggled with me over a manual typewriter complete with a tilde; the man responded to each of my offers by staggering away with a humorous, melodramatic clutch of his head before we settled on a price. I typed out what I'd written of *Fat Jammin' Joe and the Simple City Cats*, and Amy—who had read *The Ballad of Adam James*—found the new work to be better, giving me sharp advice as she went through those pages stained orange by Simona's table.

After a few weeks Simona's apartment, while an improvement on the *pension*, started to feel like what it was: temporary housing, whose curtain partition, ridiculous shower, and all-night multilingual music and talk had lost their charm. Then we met another couple, a white Californian named Leslie and her Mexican fiancé, Javier, who lived in an apartment in a suburb southwest of Barcelona called Viladecans. They needed roommates to help with their rent, and Amy and I put ourselves forward. Mostly residential, with a baker here and a barber there, Viladecans was like Barcelona's dowdy sister, its streets spreading crookedly between short, square buildings. There was one occasional sight there you couldn't find in Barcelona: a herd of sheep moving through the streets. We got along with Leslie and Javier, and the apartment was the closest thing to a home we'd found so far in Spain. The tradeoff was that the trip to and from Barcelona, by bus, wasn't one you wanted to make more than once a day. Because my teaching appointments in Barcelona were separated by hours, I would leave in the dark to take the bus to Barcelona for my first lesson, then spend sizeable chunks of the day wandering the streets of the city, stopping for a cheap lunch at one place, writing *Fat Joe* while sipping café con leche at another. Meanwhile, I was eating about a meal less per day than I had in New York, and with my constant movement I burned off most of what I did eat. One passage in Orwell's memoir *Down and Out in London and Paris*—which I read in Barcelona—has him walking down the street and seeing a poor, bedraggled, unshaven wretch coming toward him, then realizing that he is seeing a reflection in a building's glass, that the wretch is Orwell himself. Early one morning in Viladecans, as I washed up before my first lesson, I caught sight of myself in the mirror and was astonished at the emaciated body I saw. I had been skinny my whole life, but this was something else.

Sometime around the end of April, Leslie and Javier found an apartment of their own in Barcelona. Amy and I, not wanting to pay the whole rent—and be stuck in Viladecans—by ourselves, looked for another place. If you're counting, and if you're counting the *pension*, this would be our fourth living space in under five months. We had luck, or so it seemed, finding a room in an apartment in a section of northwest Barcelona called Horta, the farthest north we'd lived yet. The rent was affordable, and the neighborhood, hilly and residential, was beautiful. Our roommate and rent collector, Delores, was thirty-one; attractive, with curly, dirty-blond hair; fluent in English; and—

Later, when I tried to describe Delores to Gerald and found myself tongue-tied, my friend suggested that it was because I had never dealt with true insanity before and didn't have a frame of reference for talking about it. Maybe. But another problem was that I was trying to sum Delores up, and this was one woman who defied your attempts at summary. You're reduced to listing details, by the end of which the listener is impatient and confused and wonders who the crazy one really was. But judge for yourself:

Readers of a certain age will remember the sketch-comedy show *Laugh-In*. One segment of the show had performers popping out of windows, making quick, absurd statements, then popping in again. Delores would do that. I was alone in the kitchen one day when she appeared in the doorway and said, apropos of nothing, "Cliff, what about your ancestors? Were they slaves? What a past!"—and then was gone. Another time, Amy and I found an ice-cube tray under our bed. It wasn't ours; neither of us had put it there; it had to have been Delores. An ice-cube tray? Under our bed? Why? (Then again, since it wasn't hurting anybody, why did it bother us so? Maybe the mark of real craziness in others is that it makes you question your own sanity.) At a point when Amy and I were already having doubts about our roommate—and, to a lesser extent, ourselves—we were awakened dead in the middle of the night by a Michael Jackson album playing at full blast. Amy—courageously, I thought—went to the living room, where Delores was dancing by herself, and told her to turn that shit off.

The slowly accumulating evidence that Delores was not quite right in the head seemed stronger when we discovered what she did all day, an occupation the Spanish call *nada*. The apartment belonged, it turned out, to her parents, who ran a dry-cleaning shop not far away. Delores had her days free to steep in her own special homemade mental brew.

In his prime Muhammad Ali would overcome an opponent by dancing quickly in and out and connecting with punches that were not so much devastating as bewildering; when the other boxer was sufficiently off-balance, Ali would bring out the heavy artillery. Delores worked in a similar way. While we were still adjusting to her weirdness, she shifted from that to hostility. Worse, we didn't know from one day to the next whom we would get: the friendly but weird Delores, or the other one. A perfect example: we told her that some married friends of ours—Martha Southgate, now a novelist, and her husband Jeff Phillips—were visiting Barcelona, and asked if it was okay if they stayed at the apartment. Delores smiled sweetly, as if to say, *Why wouldn't it be okay?*, and answered, "Of course." A day or so before Martha and Jeff arrived, we mentioned their visit, and Delores seemed surprised; when we reminded her of our earlier conversation, she said, "You have invented this." One night, Jeff told us, Delores poked her head in the room where they were staying and yelled something in Catalan. Another time, seeing me preparing an English lesson, Delores told me, "You shouldn't be working in this flat." I ignored her. Where logic is useless, silence is best. Even at her nicest, Delores had an unsettling quality about her; she would ask Amy and me questions about ourselves, not in the casual way of most roommates, but with a seeming desperation to hear something, anything, that would distract her from the chaos inside her head.

Amy and I tried to ignore the things Delores said and did, but we couldn't ignore the situation we were in. We saw that we couldn't go on living where we were, a realization that brought up questions about our adventure in Spain—and about the direction of our lives. Even if we had the energy to move to yet another place in Barcelona, and even if the move turned out okay, what would be the point? We had proved that we could get by in Spain, but getting by was all we seemed able to do. I turned twenty-eight in Spain, Amy twenty-nine; we weren't in our post-college phase anymore—we were post–post college, heading toward thirty. If we weren't working out plans for the future, and we weren't particularly enjoying our time overseas, and I wasn't making Baldwinesque discoveries, then what, exactly, were we doing? Our original plan had been to spend a year in Spain; sometime around June we decided to shorten it to eight months.

And we made another decision that June. In five months we had been through more tough times together than some couples face in five years, but our feelings for each other had only gotten stronger; whatever else was going on, and whatever else there was yet to face, we realized we wanted to do it together. One night, as we sat in our favorite restaurant—the creperie—I asked a question. Amy, it seems, was no materialist: a skeletal man without a job or even a home waiting back in the States had proposed marriage, and she didn't think for a second before saying yes. We immediately told our friend José, the waiter, who grinned like a madman and brought us free drinks. We went home smashed and happy. (After I phoned my family with the news, Wanda wrote a letter saying they had told Grandma that Amy and I were getting married. Her response: "I thought they *was* married!")

Our stay in Spain got even shorter after Amy heard some news. Chris and Elizabeth Carduff were moving with their baby daughter out of their Park Slope, Brooklyn, apartment—where Amy had thrown me the surprise party for my short story "Judgment"—and into a place two floors above it. Their old apartment, which Amy loved, would be vacant by August 1. Amy quickly wrote a letter to the management company, and with a recommendation from Chris (who was to become a good friend of mine), we got the apartment.

Now it was just a matter of when to leave Barcelona. We had come on January 4; I convinced Amy that we should stay until July 4, so we would always be able to say we'd lasted half a year. To reduce the amount of stuff we would have to carry, I decided to sell the manual typewriter with the tilde—a move I regret to this day—taking it back to the man who had sold it to me. I expected to engage in another round of good-natured haggling, but he made an offer in a tone that clearly meant, *Take it or leave it.* I took it—and took his attitude as a sign that it was truly time to leave the country. On July 4, our very own Independence Day, Amy and I said goodbye to our nutty roommate, goodbye to the Sagrada Familia and the Ramblas and Tibidabo, goodbye to José and the creperie, goodbye to tapas and café con leche and that delicious paella, goodbye to Spain.

We spent six days in Venice, where the Italian sun finished the job started in Barcelona, turning my medium-brown skin the color of coffee beans and Amy's brown-blond hair platinum. Our next stop was London; for a week there we camped with Amy's expatriate Oberlin pal Tracy Chevalier—who a few years later would write *Girl with a Pearl Earring*—and her future husband, Jon. Then we flew to DC. Amy's sister, Sally, met us at the airport, her jaw dropping when she caught sight of us. She drove us to 232, where one of the first things I did was step on Ma's scale. I had gone to Spain weighing 154 pounds; I had come back at 134.

Interlude

In Djuna Barnes's celebrated but highly strange and often opaque novel *Nightwood*, there is a phrase that I found resonant: "[R]eason was inexact with lack of necessity." Those words sum up the state I was in when I returned from Spain and began life, again, in Brooklyn. In France, Baldwin had discovered that he was an American and begun to figure out his connection to his countrymen, both black and white; in Spain, I had spent half a year and dropped twenty pounds learning what Phyllis's five-year-old daughter could have told me—that I wasn't Spanish—but my discovery hadn't extended to making me feel American or telling me how I fit in among blacks and whites in my home country. That failure, I see now, occurred because of an unconscious, and therefore unexamined, belief of mine: that to be American was to be white. "America" had elected Richard Nixon in the first presidential election I was aware of, while overwhelmingly black DC, nearly alone in the country, went for George McGovern; "America," if my college experience was any indication, had never heard of James Brown, the hero of the people who produced me. I felt—again, unconsciously—that to call myself an American was to forsake being black, which I was unwilling to do; but thanks to my experiences of the past few years, I didn't feel black, either. I didn't know *what* the hell I was.

Work

Reason was inexact with lack of necessity: I hadn't figured out the race thing because I hadn't—yet—been forced to. I had more immediate concerns, such as how to help Amy pay the rent on this great apartment we'd found. Amy, who'd had enough of the publishing field, quickly landed a job with a nonprofit organization; I wasn't so quick. If I didn't know what I was racially or culturally, no one else could figure out what I was professionally. One woman at a publishing company set up an interview with me, not, it turned out, because she had me in mind for a job, but because she felt compelled to meet the person who had sent her this curiosity of a résumé. I had put in my time as an editorial assistant but wasn't an editor; had published some fiction but not sold a story collection or a novel; had landed some nonfiction writing assignments (during my Harlem days) but was hardly a journalist; had taught overseas but wasn't a teacher. What was I? Nobody seemed to know—and so, for over a year, I did the occupational equivalent of walking up a down escalator: I temped, got freelance writing assignments, worked for a literary agent out of his apartment, and held one part-time job of such unbelievable make-work that I was almost embarrassed to pick up my pay-check.

Before I could tell prospective employers what I was, it seemed, I had to know myself. I loved the written word, of course, but the question was how to turn that love into a living. As a writer? There were people with journalism degrees—a club that excluded me—who were having trouble doing that. I didn't want to be an editor like those I'd observed at Doubleday, who seemed to do everything except edit. But it occurred to me that there was one group of editors I could imagine joining, people who spent their days doing what their titles suggested. These were copyeditors, the auto mechanics of the printed page, who upheld standards of grammar, who chose between "doughnut" and "donut," who expressed in two words the meaning a writer had groped for with seven. Rich, these people were not; but the good ones could make a living.

In the summer of 1992—a couple of months after Amy and I got married—I enrolled in a copyediting course at NYU. I got an "A." From there I got freelance copyediting assignments, which helped lead me, in January 1993, to . . .

Well, let's start with its location. In his 1987 novel *The Bonfire of the Vanities*, the inimitable Tom Wolfe described the area around the courthouses in the South Bronx as a place where you risked your life just by coming out of the subway. That description was a tad out of date by the time I got there, which is not to say that the neighborhood, almost completely black and Hispanic, had become Beverly Hills East; I happened to learn while writing this chapter that the area has the highest concentration of poor people of any congressional district in the United States. So: we get off the D train at 161st Street; walking for ten minutes on River Avenue, away from the courthouses, we pass Yankee Stadium, go through an underpass, head up the steep hill of Woodycrest Avenue with low-income apartments on one side and a community center on the other, hang a left on 162nd Street, and come after a block to an eight-story building on the banks of the Harlem River that might be a hospital or—with that barbed wire—a prison, except for the olive-green lighthouse on top. We proceed down its long covered walkway, and we have arrived at a testament to things that are not dreamt of in your philosophy.

For one hundred and thirteen years, from 1898 to the economically treacherous year of 2011, when its data was acquired, its building leased, and its two hundred or so employees given severance packages and bid *adieu*, The H.W. Wilson Company published reference works that went mainly to libraries. For the most part they were indexes, series of whole books listing journal articles related to specific subjects—*Art Index, Social Science Index, Book Review Digest, Readers' Guide to Periodical Literature*. The indexers and their editors, mostly white, typically had master's degrees in library science; the stereotype is that people go to library school to avoid dealing with other people, and like many stereotypes, this one had a grain of truth to it. For each of the friendly, normal people who worked at Wilson—a well-represented group—there was one whose social cluelessness bordered on disability, once in a while sneaking across the border. There was one middle-aged, thickset, Princeton-educated man who, as he scurried up the hill to work in the mornings, would stop at every payphone to look for change; arriving, he headed straight to the sixth-floor men's room, where he would take a dirty, sweat-stained, malodorous shirt out of a plastic bag to replace the dirty, sweat-stained, malodorous shirt he was wearing. While in the men's room, he—no, we won't go there.

The company had one anomalous department, General Publications, which included a magazine started in 1940: *Current Biography*, published eleven times a year and then made into a green, hardbound yearbook. The 3,000-word articles in *Current Biography*, about famous living people in many fields, took their information from already-published sources—newspapers, magazines, and, later, the Internet. *Current Biography* would turn up in the strangest places. The average citizen would look blank or perplexed at the mention of it, but the *New York Times* cited it now and then; it was frequently quoted in examples of usage in *Webster's Dictionary*; and the news anchor Peter Jennings is reported to have said on national TV, shortly after the death of John F. Kennedy Jr., that the best profile of Kennedy he'd read was in *Current Biography*. With the title of assistant editor, I became *CB*'s copyeditor. Remember the Afro-American history book I read in third grade at my little rolltop desk? As a nine-year-old in a neighborhood of not-rich brown-skinned folks, I had labored over reports on famous people based on a previously published source; as a twenty-nine-year-old in similar surroundings, I was doing much the same. Even more remarkable was that for the first time, I was getting paid for work that I enjoyed and felt good at. On *M*A*S*H*, Henry Blake, looking ahead to leaving war-ravaged Korea for his medical practice back in Bloomington, Illinois (a journey he was never to complete), said to Hawkeye, "This place—this place which has all the attraction of a lanced boil—has given me the opportunity to do more doctoring than I can do in a lifetime back in the world." At H. W. Wilson, this dorks' paradise in the middle of a slum, I was able to do more editing than I ever would have at Doubleday, with its chic Midtown Manhattan address and Christmas parties at the Waldorf Astoria. "I really like it," I said to my wife in bed one night, and I guess that's why, through ups and downs and in various capacities—including, eventually, editor in chief of *Current Biography*—I stayed for just shy of nineteen years.

I had solved the least of my problems.

Interlude

When last we saw, the agent Faith Childs was sending *The Ballad of Adam James* around to publishers. The novel got several rejections before Faith told me she was too busy to pursue it anymore and dropped me. (I remember a letter from one publishing house: "I don't think the novel is there yet, though I do think Thompson is talented.") Meanwhile, I finished *Fat Jammin' Joe and the Simple City Cats*, which came closer to the mark without hitting it. "I to'd and fro'd about the novel," the in-house editor of Terry McMillan's anthology wrote me in a letter, "because there are so many fine things in it." Repeat that sequence of events, with slight variations, and then repeat it again, and you have the story of my novel-writing career. Me, special? Ha.

There is the old saying about a window opening when a door closes. One opened a crack for me—well, actually, I put a crack in it. But I've gotten ahead of myself.

Jazz, Fatherhood, and Albert Murray

I turned thirty in the late winter of 1993. On the very same day, sitting at my desk in the *Current Biography* offices, I got a call from Amy, who had just seen a gynecologist. When we hung up, I shivered, briefly; I was scared, and I was happy. And I was in for a confusing time, because there is nothing like approaching a milestone—fatherhood, say—for bringing up unfinished personal business.

Several weeks after that day, Amy and I went to the Manhattan apartment of one of her co-workers for a Passover Seder. The other guests included more co-workers and a woman I'll call Barbara, who was then a good friend of Amy's. My wife and I were the only non-Jews present; I was the only black guest, a scenario I was certainly used to by that point. I enjoyed the meal, and I participated in the readings, which I found interesting. It was when the eating and ceremony were over, and the after-dinner chit-chat began, that the trouble started. Barbara and one of the co-workers—I'll call her Moira, because I hate that name—began talking about the experiences they had in common because of their heritage; they even sang verses of a Jewish camp song they both remembered, a song of tradition and celebration. As the reminiscing went on, and I continued to sit quietly through it, a sadness began to overtake me, not so much because I was excluded from this conversation as because I couldn't imagine a similar one in which I would be an active participant. My black friends and I could—and sometimes did—take nostalgic jaunts in which we laughed over black fads, films, and hair-care products from the 1970s. But what was the black American equivalent of a Jewish camp song? Where, in other words, were the fondly remembered pieces of a black tradition that *didn't* make us laugh? What constituted our celebration of ourselves? Our Seder?

At some point during the discussion of Jewish camp songs, Moira said to Barbara, "It's cool that you and I just met but we have this in common." Was there really no positive tradition that all or most blacks had in common? There was, of course, Kwanzaa, an annual, not exactly widespread African-American celebration developed relatively recently—too recently for me to have embraced it as a tradition. There were, also, the trappings of the black church, the all-day-Sunday services and screaming, sweating Protestant ministers, but those were, at least ostensibly, more about Christianity than blackness—and more importantly, as a lapsed member of the staid Catholic church I couldn't claim those things as part of my story, either.

I was brooding over all this, my mood already darkening, when Moira turned to Amy and me and said, "You guys aren't holding up your end of the conversation!"

Barbara said to Moira, "Ask him about *Hill Street Blues*." This was a TV police drama Barbara and I both liked. The sad thing was her sincerity; far from being facetious, she was trying to help—which is why I wanted to hit her. *Hill Street Blues*? *This* was the source of my cultural identity, the base from which I related to other people? I felt insulted, and instead of opening up, I retreated further into my silent gloom. When, after what seemed a week, our evening together came to a close, Moira shot a mean grin in my direction and said, joking but not really, "Have something to say next time!" I am, as we know, a gentle man; I left the Seder capable of second-degree murder.

The Seder had not only made me realize that there were no traditions I held sacred: it had made me see that I knew of no sufficient basis for such traditions. Yes, there were the stories in my third-grade Afro-American history book—the stories of Benjamin Banneker, Frederick Douglass, Harriet Tubman, Sojourner Truth, George Washington Carver, Charles Drew, Martin Luther King, and others. I knew about the bravery of black soldiers in every American war since the Revolution, about the daring of the black cowboys, about the artists of the Harlem Renaissance. I was proud of those things. But they felt like fragments—not the solid ground on which a tradition rested, but that same ground after an earthquake, broken into pieces by a calamity of slavery, poverty, prejudice, and plain old bad luck. What I needed, and didn't seem to have, was something that would unite those pieces and even reconcile them with all the misery—something that would connect the dots of my heritage and show me the picture, as a Seder did for Jews. And the thing was, I couldn't draw the picture myself; it had to be there already, it had to be good and old; I could not create it because I needed to have come from it.

This was the problem I'd had in relating to other black people: if my connection to them could be threatened by things as trivial as the way I talked or the skin color of the person I was dating, it was because the connection was rooted in nothing—at least nothing I knew of—deeper than pigmentation. And *that*, in turn, was the source of my unease over being surrounded by so many white people: unlike me, they never had to question their identities. They were Americans. Some were also Jews. What was I? I knew that Afrocentric blacks felt themselves to be Africans living on American soil; I applauded their confidence and wished them well, but I did not feel myself to be one of them. I thought it regrettable, to say the least, that my link to the Motherland had been severed, but in my view the damage had been done, and was irreparable. I had never been to Africa, I spoke no African languages, I didn't know which of the many African tribes my ancestors had come from, and I felt incapable of embracing an emotional and intellectual connection that did not exist.

"Intellectual": what made all of this more than a head game was that I was about to bring a child, a biracial human being, into the world, and this kid's guide through the thicket of racial/ethnic identity would be *me*? A man still lost after three decades was going to show somebody else the way? God help this kid, and God help me. What was I doing? What had I done?

I was on the lookout, more intensely than I'd ever been, for an idea to help orient me. For that reason I recalled something I had read recently, an essay in Stanley Crouch's first collection, *Notes of a Hanging Judge*. Crouch's take on the singer Michael Jackson's mutilation of his facial features was that it echoed African customs—while, at the same time, exemplifying American self-reinvention. A black man was seen as embodying Americanness? I was intrigued. Another essay in the book mentioned a black cultural critic I had never heard of, one Albert Murray. After a long search conducted in those days before amazon.com, while Amy's belly grew bigger, I tracked down a copy of Murray's first book, *The Omni-Americans*. Thus did I add the seventh and final face to my own personal Mount Rushmore.

The Omni-Americans helped me do two things: find a definition of blackness that did not exclude me, and see how that very blackness not only didn't exclude me from Americanness—but actually *made* me American. At the heart of the American experiment was the notion of making a way where none had existed, a shining testament to that idea being the US Constitution. That determination to survive by making a new way—to improvise—had parallels in black history: for example, the Underground Railroad and the civil rights movement, which were American in both geography and spirit. Murray's work also helped me to understand how the racial distinctions we all obsess over are largely false, in a land where blacks had both shaped and been shaped by a culture Murray called "incontestably mulatto." I realized I had seen examples of this my whole life. When the father and oldest son on *The Brady Bunch* can slap five, when the boys I grew up with could turn their jacket collars up in imitation of Fonzie on *Happy Days*, when US blacks have ancestors from the same continent as descendants of southern Italians, when blacks and whites alike have Native Americans in their bloodlines, when there are whites and blacks who can trace their lineage back to Thomas Jefferson, when the first jazz was played on instruments left over from Confederate army bands (!), when there are growing numbers of biracial individuals—when all those things are true, then not only do Americans, as Murray pointed out, look like no one so much as one another: to a great extent, they *are* one another.

The ability to improvise was at the core of one of black people's major contributions to the culture of the United States and beyond, an art form that I myself, would you believe it, had already begun to embrace. Yes:

Jazz. It was both the product of, and metaphor for, the black American story—it was my old Afro-American history book set to music. Just as importantly, maybe more so, I loved the sound. I had started with Parker, Guaraldi, Rollins, and Monk, and I had picked up two landmark albums, Miles Davis's *Kind of Blue* and John Coltrane's *Giant Steps*; now, I began reaching for jazz records as if for life rafts, which in a sense they were. I checked out the marvelous sax work of Ben Webster, Cannonball Adderley,

Stanley Turrentine, Jackie McLean, Dexter Gordon, Lucky Thompson, Joe Henderson, Wayne Shorter, and the great rivals, the Romulus and Remus of the tenor sax, Coleman Hawkins and Lester Young; felt excited listening to the drumming of Art Blakey, Max Roach, Buddy Rich, Philly Joe Jones, and Tony Williams; listened raptly to the rocketing trumpet solos of Freddie Hubbard, Booker Little, Charlie Shavers, Howard McGhee, Roy Eldridge, and Dizzy Gillespie; got carried to other planes by the piano work of Kenny Barron, Jaki Byard, and Bill Evans. I began keeping track of which sidemen had played with which bandleaders—Johnny Hodges with Ellington, Charlie Rouse with Monk, Johnny Dodds with Armstrong—and began to distinguish among the sounds of different saxmen, trumpeters, drummers, and pianists as among different human voices: there was the sweetness of Cannonball, the earthiness of Webster, the ethereality of Young. I began to search out great but less-remembered players: Wardell Gray, Ike Quebec, Teddy Charles, and more.

Meanwhile, I pursued Albert Murray. I read his other books, including *Stomping the Blues*; his wonderful work of literary theory, *The Hero and the Blues*; and his Scooter novels, which are not my favorites of his works but are worth a look, especially the first two. On the semi-pretext of interviewing and writing about Murray for *Current Biography*, where I was by then an associate editor, I tried everything I could think of to get in touch with him before resorting in desperation to an approach so obvious it seemed doomed to fail: calling Directory Assistance. Next thing I knew I was talking to him. In the spring of 1994 (two years before Henry Louis Gates wrote that definitive profile of him for the *New Yorker*), when I was thirty-one and he was about to turn seventy-eight, I went to the eighth floor of a high-rise in my old stomping grounds of Harlem, where Murray lived with Mozelle, his wife of five decades. The Murrays' apartment, not enormous but comfortable, was filled with two things: books and talk, most of the latter supplied by Murray himself. The Alabama-born Murray had been a major in the air force, in which he taught aerodynamics and military strategy, before moving to New York and immersing himself in the life of the mind—taking up where he had left off with his great pal Ralph Ellison at Tuskegee. He befriended the artist Romare Bearden, ghost-writing—according to Gates—the lectures Bearden gave at Yale at Gates's invitation; he hung out for years with

Count Basie, preparatory to writing the bandleader's autobiography. Murray, this handsome near-octogenarian, seemed to have seen, done, read, heard, and thought it *all*, and if he left anything out while holding forth rapidly in his high voice, I don't know what it was.

Feeling myself to be in the presence of greatness, having found something akin to those long-ago talks with Phyllis, I went back to his place whenever new fatherhood allowed, taking advantage of Murray's generosity with his time. We drank his Armagnac while he read to me passages from Frederic Prokosch's novel *The Asiatics* and Hermann Broch's novel *The Death of Virgil*; as a co-creator of Jazz at Lincoln Center, he invited me to a concert, where I sat between him and Stanley Crouch (they were still talking then), the two of them trading musical observations across my lap. One evening at his apartment Murray told me that George A. Dorsey's book *Why We Behave Like Human Beings* had informed his own "anthropological orientation," which underlies his work: a belief in the importance of myth and ritual—ritual formed by the means of survival, with art and culture being the stylization of that process. "Art," Murray said, "comes out of play based on survival." (Jazz, anyone?) In 1997, when Murray received the Langston Hughes Award from the City College of New York, he recommended me to write and deliver a tribute to him, which I did, proudly, with Amy in the audience.

Like many very smart people, and like many old people, my friend could be impatient and cranky. More than once he sent me across the room to his extensive bookshelves to find a volume related to a point he was making. "Not that one," he might say. "*Look* under the *god damn*—"

"Stop yelling at me!" I told him one day, and to my great surprise he did, his face that of a scolded and repentant little boy as he said softly, "Okay." Another time, handing him a book I had found under duress, I said, "It's a good thing I like you."

"It's a good thing I like *you*," he said, smiling, laughing that rich, throaty laugh.

What about that child we were about to bring into the world? She arrived on a Friday night in Manhattan, seven pounds and five ounces and, in my first sighting of her, a deep shade of purple. Her name lent itself to a number of nicknames, one of which was The Pie. I remember taking her to a pedia-trician for her first post-hospital check-up; at one point the doctor was out of the room, and Amy and I stood over The Pie, who was lying naked on a table, gazing up at us. "Don't you love her?" I said, and I thought how, when she was old enough, I would have a story to tell this little girl.

Interlude

The occasion may have been Wayne's moving out of 232; or maybe it was when Phyllis turned twenty-one, which meant that she, Wayne, and Wanda were all of legal age. Whatever was going on, my father said aloud, though mostly to himself, "I'll look up one day, and all my children'll be gone."

He must have repeated my response to everyone he knew. "Just look down," I said, "and I'll be here."

On a sunny morning in May of 2008, Phyllis's daughter Elinor graduated from NYU. The ceremony was held at Yankee Stadium, in the Bronx. There is a photograph, taken by Elinor's older sister, Emily—a lawyer by then—of four Thompsons sitting together in the stands, looking sideways and smiling at the camera: Wayne, at fifty-nine a retiree of the US Postal Service and the assistant pastor at his church; Wanda, fifty-seven, an administrator of two-decades'-plus standing at Children's Hospital in DC—*and* a Baptist minister, at a church she would later pastor; Phyllis, fifty-five, a judge on the DC Court of Appeals; and your humble correspondent, forty-five, wearing wire-frame glasses so his once-sharp eyes could make out what was happening down on the field.

When the graduation ceremony was over we had lunch on the Grand Concourse and then took a short bus ride up the hill to a place no one in our party besides me had ever seen: the offices of The H.W. Wilson Company. "Heads up," I said to my crew of six or seven twenty-something writers, sitting at their cubicles, when we walked in. I made introductions—which felt like one of those dreams in which completely separate elements of your life converge—and then showed my family to my office. Phyllis saw proofs of the next issue of *Current Biography* on my desk and commented on them; Wanda asked where we got photographs for the magazine.

Wayne, though, zeroed in on something on my windowsill: a small, framed, black-and-white photo taken in Virginia in the 1940s. The photo shows ten or so people in what looks like a shack, with an old-fashioned ice box, sitting or standing around a table, eating, drinking, and talking. I can identify only a few of them. Uncle Manson sits to the far right, bent over a plate of food, his hair fuller and darker than I ever saw it in real life. Uncle Harry stands at the left. Between them is a man I never met: my father in his twenties, seated, wearing a dark shirt and light-colored suspenders, holding a coffee cup, mouth open to show an imperfect set of teeth, and looking as if he's talking—talking about what, I am a world, an age, a lifetime away from ever knowing.

Workings of the Heart

A strange but unavoidable fact about working life is that often, when you do one job well enough, you get moved to another one, for which you have no training—while those who are not as good at your first job are left to continue doing it.

In the mid-1990s there was a re-organization within H.W. Wilson, which was not pretty but ultimately benefited me. The benefits were hard to see at first. Given a barely discernible raise, I was taken out of *Current Biography*, which I loved, and placed for two years in the larger General Publications department, where I supervised and edited the work of four writers—a pair of whom were considerably older than me and were, as my boss described them, "two of the biggest personnel challenges I've ever seen." I mention these events because they led me, in a way that Rube Goldberg would have appreciated, to rethink impressions I had formed at the age of ten.

So: one of those two graying folks was a man I'll call Merle; the other gets to keep her name, which was Selma Yampolsky. More than a few minutes passed between ending that last sentence and undertaking this one, because, as with my old Barcelona housemate Delores, it's hard to know where to start. Selma was gnomelike—short of stature, short, crinkly hair, short of the social graces we tend to take for granted, which are usually conspicuous only in their absence, like good acting, say, or eyebrows. It was painful, for instance, to be with Selma during group discussions at office parties. Like much social interaction, after all, group discussions have a rough choreography to them, and Selma never made the rehearsals. So she could take a conversation hostage, dragging it down a narrow path no one could or wanted to follow, going on and on about some inane topic while others studied the ice in their Diet Cokes or just drifted away. One February day I saw Selma approach my boss, look up at him with a blank face and closed mouth, and grunt twice. My boss, smiling as if in the presence of the mentally unfit—which he was—said in the most soothing voice possible, "I'm sorry, Selma, I don't understand." She explained that it was Groundhog Day, and she was a groundhog.

Before their work was placed under my editorship, Selma and Merle were themselves editors, overseeing volumes of biographical articles about authors. Now, demoted in all but name, they were writing articles. Merle proved to be good at that. Selma, it turned out, couldn't—for all her erudition—write worth beans. She composed prose in the same disordered way she spoke and thought; a paragraph supposedly summing up an author's oeuvre would be taken up with a description of one passage in one book she'd found funny. Selma and Merle were alike, though, in their frustration and bewilderment at the turn their careers had taken. Because they had me surrounded—Merle's cubicle was behind mine, Selma's in front—I got to hear all about it, the barbed comments flying like live ammo over my head. I ignored this stuff, or tried to, until I couldn't anymore, at which point I would go to their desks and tell them in essence to shut the fuck up. "I'm not some summer intern," I recall saying to Selma. "I know," she said, with her head lowered. "You're my boss." Sometimes she dispensed with the barbs and resorted to combativeness. "Now wait a minute," she said once or twice, stomping to my desk with an article I'd covered in red pencil marks, ready to go to the mat over number 3,684 of the 5,422 changes I'd made in an attempt to lend some coherence to the mess she'd turned in.

Over time Selma seemed to me alternately amusing and sad rather than aggravating. When she called me, maybe twice a week, to tell me she was running late, each time saying the exact same thing in the exact same way—"Hi, it's Selma, I'm stuck on the subway," the whoosh of a train behind her—I thought that if I listened hard I could hear the theme music to the sitcom I'd surely stumbled into. I may strain credulity by writing here, truthfully, that I came to like Selma (and Merle, too) a little. She actually respected me and my editing ability, telling me once, "You wield a mean axe." And she was not, beneath it all, a bad person. Wilson had book sales a couple of times a year, and once Selma touched my heart by presenting me with a book, *The Frog Who Wanted to Be a Singer*, which became one of my favorite things to read to The Pie. When Selma found something particularly funny she would giggle like a little girl, and I once made her do just that by recounting an old *Saturday Night Live* sketch.

None of that, of course, helped her writing. (Why hadn't she been fired long ago? Because the company didn't want to be slapped with an age-discrimination suit.) After I was put in charge of all of Wilson's biographical publications and moved to an office away from Merle and Selma, I should have been able to delegate the editing of Selma's articles to someone else, but I had a very hard time finding anyone who wasn't driven to tears—that actually happened once—by her stuff. (Selma, I heard, huffily told one person that only I was allowed to edit her work.) One day, finally, I decided enough was enough; lawsuits and children's books aside, that batty little old lady had to go. "Well," my boss said wearily, "let's build a case." I started doing that, but when we got right down to it, I had a vision of Selma in the near future living under some steps in Grand Central Station, and I couldn't, as they say, pull the trigger. Depending on your point of view, that makes me a compassionate human being or a lousy manager, but before you decide, consider the following: in 2009, when H.W. Wilson's troubles started in earnest, Selma was one of the first to be laid off. Less than a year later, sick, unable to find work, and not seeing much of a life ahead of her, she killed herself.

I have, in true Selma fashion, strayed from the point, which is this:

When I was sandwiched between Merle and Selma, other colleagues would ask me how I stood it. I think I gave the impression of calmly rising above it all. The real story was a little different. Sitting there quietly day after day, I got so tense that my occasionally wacky heartbeat got wackier on more frequent occasions, to the point where I felt like Art Blakey had a standing gig inside my chest. When I'd first felt this abnormality, I was twenty-two, single, and living in my mother's house; now, coming up on thirty-five, I was married with one child and a second on the way. I could no longer ignore my symptoms; the hour had come for hauling my black ass to a cardiologist.

You cannot, ever, predict how a thing will go. The cardiologist, Dr. Andrew Van Tosh, wasn't bothered by the heart "skips" that I had secretly worried about for over a decade; half the population, he said, develops them sooner or later—mine had started sooner, that was all. The tests did turn up something else, though: what Dr. Van Tosh called a "moderately reduced heart-muscle function." When a person has suffered a coronary, he explained, part of his heart shuts down while the rest carries on; in my case, the overall function of the muscle had been weakened. A stress test showed that my heart could rise to the occasion and get me through whatever I needed to do, but in the main, this heart of mine was no Muhammad Ali—more like Ali McGraw. The cause of this wasn't clear; a virus, maybe, or my borderline-high blood pressure. "Obviously, this isn't good news," Dr. Van Tosh said, but he added that my heart could possibly get stronger (lowering my blood pressure would help, he said), or I could also live for decades with my heart the way it was.

That second "could" cast a shadow over my mind, implying as it did another possibility, i.e., an early grave, like my father's. I shouldn't make too much of the comparison: my father was in pain a fair amount of the time, and I was not; he loved his cigarettes and had for decades, whereas I could count on the fingers of one hand the times I had smoked anything at all; I went to the YMCA regularly, and I never saw my father exercise; I had the benefit of nutrition information on food labels, while he had been raised to eat parts of the pig a lot of people would pass up if it meant starvation. In short, I was a good deal healthier than my father. But the news from Dr. Van Tosh had caused me to identify with my father to an extent: to understand, just a little, how it must have felt to be pretty sure you would not see your child grow up.

When I thought of William Dean Thompson, several men came to mind. One was the cab-driving, newspaper-devouring army veteran, the man of the world with a taste for the written word, the ageless—because dead—figure I had long wanted to share my work, thoughts, and ideas with. Another was the man I had actually spent time with, my old checkers, chess, and Scrabble companion. Still another was the middle-aged bastard out in the backyard yelling insults at his scared ten-year-old son as they played catch, the man I still wanted to give a piece of my mind. And then there was—for me—the least real Dean, the one I never met and didn't learn about until I was grown: the gambler, the one who seemed to have little control over himself. Uncle Harry, Dean's younger brother, told me that my father once nearly lost our family's house. One day when Phyllis visited New York, the two of us reminisced about the trip she, our mother, and I took to Manhattan in the summer of 1975, when I was twelve; Phyllis said, "We had money to do it, because Daddy had died." I said, "How did that bring us money?" She said, "He couldn't gamble it away."

Now, in the hologram projector of my brain, these versions of my father were superimposed on one another to form a human being, one who looked a lot like me, especially when he smiled. Then came a day when I realized we might be alike in other ways, too.

In the summer of 2001 I taught The Pie, who was then seven, to ride a bike. As huge a cliché as this is, one of the things I will hold onto on my deathbed is the image of my girl as she first took off by herself down Prospect Park West, to the cheers of two women sitting on a nearby bench. What I don't like to remember—and therefore can't, at least not very well—are the things I said to my daughter as we worked toward that glorious result. I do know that, guided by the negative example of my own childhood, I tried to keep any frustration—which I definitely felt at certain moments—out of my voice; but my daughter alone will be the judge of whether I succeeded. Let's say I did, though. Would I have succeeded if I'd been fifty-two, not thirty-eight, and in pain? Would I have been out there trying at all?

So it was a human being, not an ogre, who had played catch with me when I was ten. Like any human being, my father had some moments that were better than others, and I began to think of some of the good ones from those baseball sessions. When we progressed from playing catch to having me field pop flies hit by my father, we needed a space bigger than our backyard, so we went over the hill to the long yard next to Richardson Elementary. We were there one summer evening when we heard something striking the metal side of the school annex, very close to where we stood. It soon became clear that they were shots from a BB gun or a .22, and that someone we couldn't see was getting his jollies by firing in our direction, no doubt from a window of the nearby apartment building. To this day I wonder what I would've done in my father's place, and I like to imagine that it would've been something close to what he did. I also wish I could remember the words he shouted as he stood with his head up and his chest out, facing the apartment building. I do remember that his voice was full of defiance and empty of fear—and that when his shouts ended, so did the shots.

On the Monday evenings when we went to the field next to my school, we always came home in time to watch *Gunsmoke* together. In one episode of that long-running TV Western, the main character, Marshal Matt Dillon, was shot and went into a coma; the town madam, Kitty, sat by his bed and—as TV characters are wont to do—began talking to the unconscious lawman, reminiscing about their relationship. My father, in the tone of weary derision with which he responded to most TV shows, said to me, "I think this one's just going to be her talking, Cliff." On the face of it, God knows, this was an unremarkable moment, but the reason I have remembered it for four decades goes beyond my admittedly strange memory; it has to do with the comradely tone in my father's voice. *I think this one's just going to be her talking, Cliff*—i.e., this disappointment is one you and I will have together, an experience we will share as equals. This wasn't me letting him down at baseball; it was just Dean and his buddy Cliff, watching TV together.

My father sometimes liked to build things with me—a toy wooden barge, for instance, that we put together in the basement (and that never touched any water, come to think of it). He was much mellower during those times than when we played ball together, maybe because I was in the assistant's role and could screw up only so badly, and maybe, too, because he didn't have to push his sick body quite so much. But it seems to me now that while the irritability wasn't there, the intensity still was, as if he was trying to get in "quality" time with me while he still could, as if he was working with one eye on a clock I couldn't see.

In 2001, the year of The Pie's bike lessons and three years after my first visit to the cardiologist, I decided to have more tests done. As I awaited the results, I hoped only that my heart hadn't gotten any weaker. Then I found out that it had actually strengthened, to the point of being on the low side of normal. If I played my cards right, according to Dr. Van Tosh, I might have a long, normal life. That news had an almost stranger effect on me than the earlier news that there was a problem. I realized that in my mind I had unconsciously foreshortened my own life—because of the initial test results and, I don't doubt, because of what happened to my father; I became aware of thinking this way only when I heard that I might have a normal life span, that I might have what my father didn't, at least where I was concerned: time to see my children grow up.

It would be disingenuous, at best, to suggest that I was sorry to hear this news. I will say, though, that a small part of me was sad at the idea of an end to this dark bond, this shared sorrow, with my dead father. And the sadness stemmed from the understanding, all these years later, that my father felt a bond with me:

When I was eight years old, before our baseball sessions, my father was hospitalized briefly; one Sunday I went to the hospital with several members of my family for a visit. They visited him, anyway—children weren't allowed in the patients' rooms, so I had to stay in the waiting area. But someone, I don't remember who, thought it would be okay if I peeked into his room long enough to wave. So I crept down the hall until I was standing outside the open doorway to his room. He was sitting up in bed; when he saw me, his face broke into a big grin of surprised delight, seeming bigger still for the gap in his teeth where the plate had been. Happy for that brief, stolen glimpse of his boy, he waved at me—not a little wave, but a wave worthy of a loved one on board a ship heading out to sea.

Interlude

Life really is a jazz tune. In the beginning you play along with everybody else, stating the theme, the one you'll come back to wittingly or not, willingly or not; then comes the bridge and the break, and with the theme as a jumping-off point, you play your solo, bringing what you've learned to each new situation, trying to create something of your own; and in the end you return to the theme, facing what you've come from, and what you've done about it.

Plugdinism

My Uncle Brock died in December of 1990, while I was living in Amy's studio apartment in Park Slope and about to leave for Spain. I cried, remembering his kindness to me when I was a boy, feeling a piece of my boyhood slip away. In Barcelona a month later, I wanted to write to Aunt Catherine, Uncle Brock's widow and partner in bickering for five decades, so I called Ma from the Telefonica building to ask about that part of my aunt's address I never could keep straight. I left Telefonica in tears, having heard from Ma that Aunt Catherine had passed, too.

In early 1994 Gerald, who had left Doubleday and held other publishing jobs since then, asked to see something I had written, saying he might be able to get it published. I sent him a manuscript, attaching a note in the usual tone of our correspondence: "This shit cost money to mail. Use it or I'll hurt you." A while passed with no word from Gerald, which was not like him, but soon I forgot the whole thing. All became clear one day in the spring. Gerald, who had a wife, two children, and, it seemed, a secret life, called from his hospital bed to tell me in a trembling voice that he had AIDS. I went to see him in the hospital; he was lucid until just before the end of the visit, when he mentioned, sounding very content, his eyes closing in sleep, that Cliff had been to see him. Before I could visit him a second time, he died.

The funeral was held at a Seventh Day Adventist church, a couple of blocks from my old apartment in Harlem—the same church where, three years earlier, Gerald's mother's funeral had been held. It's hard to single out the worst thing about the service. Was it that the team of ministers seemed to know absolutely nothing about the man they were eulogizing? Was it the way they praised themselves and each other for showing up, after hinting that they'd had to think hard about it? Maybe it was how they kept calling Gerald's widow, Laura, "the wife"? Or could it have been the anti-gay joke made by one of the ministers?

Two things redeemed the funeral—the first intentional, the second not. Midway through the service, many of those in attendance got up one by one to talk about how much Gerald had helped them with their personal lives, their writing, or their careers; I stumbled through a tribute of my own. A number of people spoke movingly. When we were all done, one of the ministers, who had listened closely for anything he could use, returned to the lectern to observe that Gerald was obviously "one of the most important people in literature in the history of this nation."

Gerald could be called a lot of things; "one of the most important people in literature in the history of this nation" is not among them. And that statement made me feel just a little better about the whole proceeding, not because the minister had tried to pay Gerald a compliment, but because his attempt revealed the extent of his limitations. It seemed, then, that the ridiculousness of Gerald's funeral owed less to bigotry than to something else, something that called not for anger but for pity.

Uncle Manson passed away in 1999, though not before turning 100 and not before completing his final artwork: painting everything in the house where he lived alone—including the TV screen—white. Grandma followed him the next year, at 106, an age by which she had forgotten who I was. Uncle Nay died in 2006, at ninety-eight, and Ma the year after that, at eighty-two. My cousin Fuzzy stayed on in Uncle Nay's house, but with Phyllis and her girls—no longer girls—having long since left 232, the old Division Avenue gang was just about gone.

So much death, so much life. In 1998 Amy and I had our second child, a girl I'll call Lou, part of one of her nicknames—the adorable Lou, with the funny sticking-up black hair on her tiny little head. I knew that Lou was the last child I would bring into the world. From a purely biological standpoint, the function of my life was complete. Earlier that year I had gotten the first report, the bad one, from my cardiologist.

It was not a coincidence, I think now, that 1998 was also the year I started keeping the notebooks. Old West figures, Matt Dillon from *Gunsmoke,* carried pistols on their hips to ward off death; for the same reason, though I didn't think of it that way at the time, I started keeping a notebook in my hip pocket. That sounds funny—it *is* funny—but it is not a joke. The notebook is always a Clairefontaine; I tried a Moleskine, which looks cooler, but those wear out too easily. And, anyway, Clairefontaine has come out with cooler-looking notebooks recently. What do I put in the notebooks? Things I hear or read about that are related to what I love: books, jazz, film, art. Let's say it's Saturday morning and I'm reading the *New York Times Book Review;* in a piece about a book by a writer I know, I come across the name of one I don't. I set down my coffee, out comes the notebook, and in goes that previously unknown writer's name. The process works the same way for jazz records, saxophonists, trumpeters, pianists, films, filmmakers, and painters whose names I don't recognize. Partially filled notebook in hand, I cruise the shelves of Strand Books, comb the listings of film-revival houses and museums, and search the items on iTunes (formerly, the racks of Tower Records) on a quest for the things I've written down—these guests at the party, the party of art; some turn out to be wonderful, others less so, but that's a party for you, and even the weaker works are not a waste of time: you've checked them out, you know what they're about, and you never know how some nugget from one of them will connect to something else. And the connections are where the real magic lies.

An example of the magic at work:

One day in 1999 I sat in my office at *Current Biography*, the brown waters of the Harlem River visible out the window behind me, the window to my right giving a view of Bronx rooftops, The Pie's kindergarten artwork on the wall in front of me, a steaming mug of black coffee on my desk, beside the article I was editing. In the article's research packet, I came across a piece in the *Nation* that mentioned in passing the group of left-leaning New York intellectuals of the 1930s and 1940s. I was only dimly aware of the existence of this group, and most of the names listed in connection with it were not familiar to me at all: Lionel Abel, Philip Rahv, Dwight Macdonald, Meyer Shapiro, R. P. Blackmur, Harold Rosenberg. Their names went into the notebook, and soon I bought Abel's memoir *The Intellectual Follies*, which was great fun; Macdonald's collection *On Movies*, which I still pick up from time to time; and Macdonald's *Against the American Grain*, from which I profited in several ways. In addition to being a witty, provocative book, it led me to read *Meditations*, by the stoic philosopher and Roman emperor Marcus Aurelius, just about the only work of philosophy I've found to have meaning for actual, everyday life. Meanwhile: I wrote in my notebook at various times the names Johnny Coles (jazz trumpeter) and Clifford Jordan (saxophonist), and I made note of a newly unearthed Charles Mingus recording, *Cornell 1964*, whose personnel includes Coles and Jordan, and whose cuts include one called "Meditations." As I listened to Mingus's "Meditations," it struck me that his thirty-one-minute work had much—besides its title—in common with Marcus Aurelius's masterpiece, chiefly an expression of imperviousness to adversity; and the realization became the core of an essay that brought me actual money.

How does any of this ward off death? It allows my knowledge, and therefore my mind, to grow, and a thing that is growing does not die. Someday, of course, all will go white—the white of Moby-Dick, of Uncle Manson's final artwork, of the abyss, of nothingness. But my plan is that when death comes, it will catch me in the middle of learning something.

The plentitude of works to explore, the continuous possibility of the magic of connections—this is what excites me. One good thing about this: it does not depend on the judgment of the outside world. When I am caught up in this feeling, and on a good day I am, I describe myself as being "plugged in," and so I coin a word for this feeling, this state, this love of artistic connections, this one-person school: *Plugdinism*. Nothing comes from nothing. Tom Wolfe, given credit for the advent of New Journalism, pointed instead to a 1962 article about Joe Louis by Gay Talese, who had had the audacity to begin his nonfiction account with, would you believe it, dialogue. The spark for Plugdinism was probably a 1983 *Village Voice* essay by Stanley Crouch, "Body and Soul," reprinted in *Notes of a Hanging Judge*. In it Crouch observed the way in which the artist Giotto had upended tradition by focusing on the individual rather than the setting in his paintings. "In his own way," Crouch wrote, "Louis Armstrong did the same. He discovered that his powers of imagination could stand alone, with the clarinet and the trombone of the conventional New Orleans band silenced, no longer need-ed to express the intricate and subtle musicality provided by the multilinear antiphonal style." Crouch went on to write of "relaxing into the thought of how much of my own experience had been clarified by exposure to foreign forms."

I wrote earlier about cracking a window, and Plugdinism was the rock I threw. That necessitated making room in my writing life—also known as my lunch break at the H. W. Wilson Company—for essays. For years I looked on nonfiction writing as a chore, a dry exercise, separate from the precious realm of creativity, i.e., fiction—which explains a few of the grades I got on papers at Oberlin; in my thirties, though, I found myself drawn to writing essays, and the more of them I read, the more I came to understand the skill, the insight, the—yes—creativity that often goes into them and the power a good essay can have. A longtime friend of mine, a short-story specialist, once said that a capable fiction writer could produce a personal essay in her sleep; my response is that if you can turn out a work to match Baldwin's "Equal in Paris," or Orwell's "Such, Such Were the Joys," or Gerald Early's "Dreaming of a Black Christmas," or Ian Frazier's "Canal Street," or Gayle Pemberton's "The Hottest Water in Chicago" in your sleep, you ought to spend more time in bed. Plugged In–ness, and reflections on my own expe-riences, led me to set down my thoughts, and to my great fortune, a few people—including the redoubtable Wendy Lesser, founder of *The Three-penny Review*; Michael Simms and Caroline Tanski of Autumn House Press; the nonfiction guru Phillip Lopate; and the members of the 2013 Whiting Writers' Award committee—responded to what I wrote.

Before I could make those treasured connections among the arts, I had to investigate those arts individually:

There were books. For nineteen years, while living in Brooklyn, I com-muted by subway to the Bronx. To have even a rudimentary understanding of New York City geography is to know that's a bit of a haul. Those stretches of slow reading on the D train and, later, the 4 train, strap-hanging in my fedora, were my real literary education. I read books ranging from the *Iliad*, the *Odyssey*, and the *Aeneid* to the works of Wallace Thurman, Jessie Red-mon Fauset, and Rudolph Fisher, to those of bell hooks, Cornel West, and Michael Eric Dyson, to those of Jane Austen, Thomas Hardy, Willa Cather, Thomas Mann, Theodore Dreiser, Fran Ross, Bernard Malamud, Alfred Kazin, Robert Warshow, Susan Sontag, Frederick Exley, Kazuo Ishiguru, Thomas Bernhard, Alfred Appel, Paul Beatty, Nikky Finney, Jonathan Lethem, and many, many more, books, books, books, each one pointing to two, six, a dozen, an infinite number of others I needed to read, a source of comfort and anguish. When the used books I bought fell apart, I was almost happy, because I could tape them up and keep reading—sending them like patched-up soldiers back into the battle to expand my knowledge, to advance against the enemy—ignorance—even as the enemy revealed more of itself. And in the course of all this I developed a criterion for measuring the greatness of a novel: how well it deals, however obliquely, with the quartet made up of those cruel snickering brothers time and death, their twisted kid sister, randomness, and their silent, cold-eyed father, meaninglessness.

When Grandma died I went with my mother and siblings to a funeral home in DC to discuss arrangements. On the wall of the funeral home was a framed portrait of a person I took to be the founder; the painting, showing the man in a blue suit and tie, was innocuous in almost every way, and might have hung inconspicuously in a bank, except for the slightly unusual fact of the man's being black and the very unusual expression on his face. With knitted-together eyebrows and burning eyes, he looked like a maniac, the painting itself—in this otherwise normal setting—like something in a dream or a Kafka novel. I had this painting in mind when, in late 2003, at age forty, I began to write a novel about a nineteen-year-old black male, Lester, who lives with his middle-class family in DC. Lester has been retarded and mute his whole life, a docile kid with a continuously placid expression; that expression changes to one of madness—like that of the man in the painting—on the day he begins, because of a rare set of neurological circumstances, to rap at the top of his lungs about life with his family. The family is the real subject of the novel: they must deal with this new development, as they have had to contend with Lester for nineteen years. I had written quite a bit of this novel, titled *Signifying Nothing*, when I realized two things. One was how much, theme- and character-wise, it has in common with Faulkner's *The Sound and the Fury* (even their titles have the same source); when I became aware of that, I began dropping allusions to Faulkner's novel, little in-jokes, here and there. The second thing I realized, in writing about this family that must constantly arrange itself to accommodate one member, was who Lester really is: Grandma.

With *Signifying Nothing*, I was convinced—I still am—that I had finally solved the puzzle of how to write a novel. Some of the literary agents I contacted agreed with me. What they didn't agree with was that I had written a novel that could be marketed successfully, as accomplished as some of them found it to be. Nonetheless, with *Signifying Nothing*, I became—the proof is on Amazon.com—a published novelist. Okay, so the publisher was me.

There were paintings. In 1999 Phyllis's daughter Emily graduated from high school. At a large celebration dinner in a DC restaurant, I gave Emily a present from Amy, The Pie, Lou, and me: a large print of a 1939 painting, *Couple in a Café*, by the black artist William Johnson. The painting, with its black outlines, bold colors, and misshapen body parts, shows a well-dressed black couple in nice hats having a drink at a small table. In deceptively childlike fashion, the painting sums up the couple's relationship. Her arm is around him, one of her red-gloved hands gripping his shoulder, as if holding him in place; below the table, her other hand clutches a table leg, possibly a stand-in for what she'd rather be clutching. Her eyes are trained on him; he, meanwhile, looks thoughtful, his eyes on something (someone?) we can't see. A purse sits at the very edge of the table, seemingly about to fall off—situated, in other words, as precariously as the couple's romance.

After presenting Emily with the print, I was silently annoyed at overhearing an exchange between a real-life couple in our party. The man asked what I had given my niece; the woman told him it was a cartoon. I realized I was more annoyed with myself than with the woman, because of my inability to explain to either one of us why this was a not a cartoon but, dammit, a painting. Then, later, I wondered if the distinction really mattered, and the question led to an insight.

In 2008, after several years of sporadically scratching the old drawing itch by doing pastel sketches, I began painting in acrylics—a lot: still lifes, scenes in bars and cafes, attempts at landscapes, more still lifes. Also in 2008, in the thick of what Amy and I had designated as our young family's travel years, we spent a week in England. Off by myself in London one afternoon, I went to the Tate Modern and the Courtauld Gallery, notebook and pen in hip pocket, feeling—at age forty-five—like an eight-year-old with a thousand-dollar Toys R Us gift certificate. I gazed at those wonderful late-nineteenth and early-twentieth-century paintings, furiously writing down names of works and artists; I had done the same earlier that year, when Amy and I went for my birthday to the one-of-a-kind Barnes Museum, then in its original home, outside Philadelphia. As I studied the paintings that truly excited me, paintings with vivid colors and simple, representational forms, I saw that while they were not cartoons, my appreciation of them stemmed from my boyhood love of comics: the simple forms of Charles Schulz's *Peanuts*, the exciting colors in Stan Lee's *Origins of Marvel Comics*, first glimpsed, fleetingly, in that mall bookstore all those years ago. The paintings of Maurice de Vlaminck, Raoul Dufy, André Derain, Kees van Dongen, Alexej Jawlensky, and Georges Rouault, like Johnson's *Couple in a Café*, represent the extension and refinement, the ultimate expression, of the aesthetic I began to form while reading the comics Wayne left behind in the basement of 232. I admire the great works of the pre-nineteenth-century masters—Ingres, say, or Caravaggio—and God knows I couldn't paint anything like them, but you can have them. I find their perfection boring, because it asks nothing of me beyond admiration. On the other side of that coin, you can have a lot of conceptual art, too, because it asks everything—the only evidence of talent (beyond a talent for hucksterism) coming from the creative interpretations of critics duped into taking that crap seriously. But the figures in Matisse's paintings, for example the woman in *Laurette in a Green Robe* and the girl in *Nono LeBasque*, are people I recognize, brought to life by my own experiences as well as the masterful, *suggestive simplicity* of Matisse's style.

One Christmas Amy replaced the tied-together wood scraps I'd been using for an easel with the real thing, probably the greatest gift I've received since my old drafting table. I like nothing in this world better than sitting at the easel, painting, with Amy, The Pie, and Lou in the room, chatting with me while, say, the Mets game is on, reminding me of those days when I drew the Telstar in the company of my sisters. If I'm any judge, I paint better than I drew, maybe because the lines needed in drawing, the sense of this-ends-here, that-ends-there, make less sense to me than the possibility, in painting, of murky areas, of one thing becoming another.

There were films. In the mid-1990s I rented a Martin Ritt movie from 1961, *Paris Blues*, with Paul Newman and Sidney Poitier playing jazz musicians and Louis Armstrong appearing in a cameo role. I enjoyed it while having, as they say, issues with it, which I explained in an essay. Before sending the essay to *The Iowa Review*, which published it, I tried a place I'd found in the *Writers' Market*, a New York–based film-geek journal called *Cineaste*. Though the editors there couldn't use my piece "for a lot of reasons," as one of them told me, they were impressed enough to assign me to write about other things, usually works by black filmmakers—which is how I came to explore and review the wonderful films of Charles Burnett, whose *To Sleep with Anger* is one of my all-time favorites.

One day in 1999 I emailed several of *Cineaste's* editors, Leonard Quart, Dan Georgakas, Cynthia Lucia, and the magazine's founder and editor in chief, Gary Crowdus—who are all as friendly as they are knowledgeable about film—and asked for guidance in what to watch; I had always loved movies, I told them, and I was proud to write for *Cineaste*, and to feel worthy of doing that I wanted to have a more solid grounding in the classics of film. Gary and Dan laughed me off, telling me to simply watch what I was interested in, but Lenny and Cindy took me seriously. Cindy pointed me mostly to foreign films; while Lenny did throw in "all of Wajda" (the Polish director), his list comprised mostly American movies of the 1930s, '40s, and '50s, some of them well known, some fairly obscure: *Stagecoach, Fury, The Awful Truth, Odds Against Tomorrow, A Walk in the Sun, Crossfire, Force of Evil,* and more. (*Odds Against Tomorrow* is terrific, with a sly, smooth Harry Belafonte, with Robert Ryan bringing rare gravitas to the role of a true bastard, and with a very young Wayne Rogers, later of *M*A*S*H* fame, whose character has a brief, very unfortunate, and very memorable encounter with Ryan's.) I investigated most of both lists, kept my notebook handy for names of other films and filmmakers I came across, and checked out things I already knew to be classics—warhorses like *Jules and Jim* and *The 400 Blows*, for example. (I had frequently seen both of those listed in the *Washington Post TV Week* when I was growing up, always, always playing on those snowy UHF stations like 32 and 45. What could they possibly be about? *The 400 Blows*, in my boyhood imagination, had a big, beefy character who must endure a lot of punches to his stomach.) I rounded up the other usual suspects—Eisenstein, Renoir, De Sica, Antonioni, Bergman,

Godard, Visconti, Fellini—before hunting down somewhat more obscure films, such as Ousmane Sembene's *Black Girl*, Kon Ichikawa's *Fires on the Plain*, Dusan Makavejev's *Man Is Not a Bird*, Claude Chabrol's *Le Beau Serge* and *Les Bon Femmes*, Ermano Olmi's lovely, sad *Il Posto* . . .

Fading traces of Spanish aside, I speak one language. Because the images and words (subtitles) were separated for me in the foreign films I watched, I paid particular attention to the images, which the makers of those films did, too, more than many of their American counterparts. There was the black ink purposely spilled on white pages, and the white hand later placed on the spiller's black hair, in Antonioni's *L'Avventura*; there was the final, achingly sad shot of the aged father in Yasujiro Ozu's *Late Spring*; there was the long tracking shot of highway carnage in Godard's *Weekend*; there was the sequence of a boy running hand-in-hand with the girl he likes but doesn't know how to get close to in Olmi's *Il Posto*, the kind of moment that is too rare in American films, with their rush to make the Main Point—and exactly the kind of youthful moment that you might realize, in retrospect, was among the most special of your own rushed life. And there were films, foreign and American, that expanded my view of what was possible in the medium: John Cassavetes' *Husbands*, Chantal Akerman's *Jeanne Dielman*, Bergman's *Scenes from a Marriage*, the husband's homecoming scene in Fassbinder's *Marriage of Maria Braun*, and just about anything by Godard, as thoroughly god-awful as some of that man's movies are. That occasional awfulness doesn't stop me and the writer Thomas Rayfiel, my great friend and drinking companion and fellow Park Slope parent, from going to Godard movies whenever they come to our favorite revival house, Film Forum. I can't speak for Tom, but Godard's films have an inimitable way of making me feel that something fascinating is *about to* happen, a quality than can carry me through some pretty dull stretches; they're sort of like life that way. As we were stepping outside one night after watching I-forget-which Godard film, Tom said to me, "Well, that wasn't as bad as some of the others."

There were jazz records. Those thrilling trumpet solos of Freddie Hubbard, Booker Little, Howard McGhee, those winding, roaming sax solos of Sonny Rollins, Stan Getz, Sonny Stitt, aware of the melody but exploring the possibilities of the chords, like someone staying parallel to the main road but banging into every garbage can in the alley—this is the sound of curiosity, of discovery, of the joy of the search. This is like the tour of New York that takes in not just the Empire State Building and the Staten Island Ferry but the Bronx hole-in-the-wall that makes the world's best Reuben sandwiches, the outdoor all-female Brooklyn production of *Lord of the Flies*, the epic battle being waged on a chessboard in a shop in Greenwich Village. This is what the notebooks are about.

And there are the connections. Those polyphonous, cacophonous, glorious big-band jazz compositions of Charles Mingus are like the wide-angle shots in the works of the American filmmaker Robert Altman, which take in so much and so many at once. And jazz is like foreign film, too, sometimes pausing, in the course of interpreting one melody (the Main Point), to slip in part of another, as the highway carnage scene in *Weekend* and the boy and girl running in *Il Posto* nearly stand alone in the films they inhabit. Or jazz is like modern painting: as the saxophonist Lester Young *suggests* chords with his simple, graceful lines rather than mapping them out, like my beloved Coleman Hawkins, so do Matisse's simple brush strokes suggest the character of a face and the nature of a personality. And Young's work is like literature, like the work of Hemingway, whose sentences are powered by what they omit. All the interconnectedness excites me in the way I was once excited by the Marvel Comics heroes' wandering into one another's stories.

I am not going to be so sappy, so completely simple-minded, as to suggest that these connections between jazz on the one hand and painting, film, and literature on the other—between a black-created art form and other forms—point to a thread linking all of humanity on a high plane; I am not going to be so utterly naïve and childlike as to propose that these links demonstrate the unimportance of race, the folly of distinctions based on superficial characteristics. I am not going to do that. Okay, yes I am. I am going to be so cringe-inducingly earnest as to write here that the divisions that we, all of us, so habitually reinforce are poisonous to our souls. My late friend Gerald once told me that he refused to be the only moral person in a country rife with racism. I understand that perfectly. And yet I am prepared to be, or at least try to be, the person he would not. Call me an Uncle Tom, call me a white folks' nigger—I've heard it all before. I do not say any of this to benefit the white man, to salve anyone's rightly troubled conscience. If I am lecturing anyone, and I seem to be, then whites are well represented among the lecturees. So are blacks. So are certain Asians and Jews and Hispanics I've met. Basically, I'm fed up with us all. Harold Melvin and Mr. Moten put it best: *Wake up, EVERYBODY!*

There are certain things I'm not qualified to talk about. The greatest contemporary race-related atrocity, from my humble viewpoint, is the channeling of so many young blacks and Hispanics from poor families into schools ill-equipped to help them, into consequent ill-preparedness for higher education and good-paying work, into resulting illegal activity, and, finally, into the hands of a racist criminal-justice system and a profit-driven prison system. And as recent events have made painfully clear, people of color do not always have to break laws for those systems to descend on them, sometimes fatally. There are better and better-trained minds than mine working on that problem, which really comprises several problems. The things I want to mention instead may seem hopelessly small and trivial by comparison, until we consider the unconscious attitudes they suggest; and, as the old saying goes, look after the pennies and the dollars will look after themselves.

So: several years ago, in separate, unrelated episodes, the celebrities Whoopi Goldberg and Montel Williams—who are, as hardly need be said, black—made statements objecting to particular instances of anti-black racism. The reaction to their statements, from both blacks and whites I know personally (one of the whites is a psychiatrist), was: what are *they* doing objecting to racism, when one of them (Whoopi) is dating a white person and the other (Montel) is married to one? Let's think about this a moment. Whoopi and Montel were treated like known Nazis who had had the gall to object to acts of anti-Semitism. In this analogy, anti-Semitism is to Nazism as anti-black racism is to interracial romance. This makes sense only if we decide that dating or marrying a person of another race necessarily constitutes an insult to, and rejection of, one's own race. If you accept that idea, stop reading. If you don't, consider this: shouldn't Whoopi and Montel be seen as having *more* credibility on the subject of anti-black racism, not less, since they obviously don't hate all whites and are not the type of black people who holler "racism" every time the sky clouds over? So badly has our obsession with race impaired our humanity and our logic that Whoopi and Montel were taken to task because they treated other humans as humans rather than as representatives of a particular race. Some will say that the opposite was true—that they were open to whites *because* they were white, reflecting a hatred of themselves and other blacks. But if that's so, then why did they object to anti-black racism? They exhibited both an openness to other kinds of people and a readiness to look out for their own. Some appear to consider that hypocrisy. I call it virtue. (It's what Linus would do!)

That's the kind of virtue my friend Gerald displayed one day when, after he had complained to me for years about anti-black racism, he said, "Lately I've been more into feminist issues than black issues." It is the virtue my sister Phyllis displayed as a judge on the DC Court of Appeals, when, sensitive to prejudice in part because of her experiences as a black woman, she wrote an opinion successfully defending gay marriage in the District of Columbia. It is the virtue displayed by Andrew Goodman and Michael Schwerner.

That was the virtue I found missing in a fellow attendee at the rally for the twenty-fifth anniversary of the March on Washington. There were numerous speakers, of whom I remember two: Jesse Jackson, dressed all in black and firing up the crowd; and a woman who devoted part of her speech to gay rights. While she was talking, one of my fellow attendees, the same color as me, pointedly walked away, wearing a smile that was not a smile and shaking his head. Another time, I argued with a black male friend who insisted that blacks have it worse than women. Nothing is stupider or sadder to me than this kind of argument—over who wins the victimhood award: middle-class blacks or poor whites? Poor whites or women? Women or gays? Gays or Jews? Jews or Hispanics or Asians? If I were a rich, misogynistic, anti-immigration, anti-Semitic white supremacist, nothing would make me happier than these arguments, which I would foster with every scrap of deviousness in my arsenal. I am saying nothing that Jesse Jackson didn't say, in essence, in his speech ("Your patch isn't big enough!") at the 1988 Democratic National Convention; if I had my way, we'd all listen to that speech every night before bed.

A few years ago I went to the movies to see *Antwone Fisher*, the true story of a black man who was abandoned by his mother as a child, then endured years of abuse and struggle before finding the other members of his large, loving extended family. When the movie was over, I had no more tears left to shed. Even so, one line spoken by the title character struck me as curious at best. Fisher, a Navy man, has an argument with a fellow black shipmate, in effect calling him two-faced, and saying, "Either you tryin' to hang out with the brothers or you tryin' to hang with the white boys, man." What, I thought, would be said about an ostensibly sympathetic white character who spoke that line? And yet if anyone, anywhere, mentioned that bit of dialogue, it wasn't in my presence; if any reviewer picked up on it, I missed the review. I had one of those moments of *Am I crazy, or is everyone else?* A person is accused of being two-faced, and the evidence presented, to which no one objects, is that he has friends of different races? Two black people—Whoopi and Montel—make statements against racism, and we attack them; a black character makes a racist statement, and people don't care, if they even notice. I went home from the movie and composed an email message, which I intended to send to every black person I knew. A couple of its breathless, wild-eyed lines went something like, "Making judgments about a person based on skin color is wrong, and it is always wrong. IF SLAVERY AND ITS AFTERMATH HAVE NOT TAUGHT US THAT, THEN WE HAVE LEARNED NOTHING WORTH KNOWING." Then a while passed, I cooled down some, the email message stayed in "Draft," and—depending on your point of view—I either came to my senses or chickened out. But I did want to hear what one particular person thought of the whole thing.

A man named Amadou Diallo was gunned down by police in New York in 1999; a different man with the same name is my first cousin once removed on my mother's side, five years and eight months younger than me. Amadou and his family used to visit 232 when I was growing up, and for many years I thought of him as a cute little kid. Then came the day in 1991, shortly after my return from Spain, that I ran into Amadou in Park Slope. That cute little kid was now a grown man of great intelligence, warmth, and humor, and we struck up a friendship that has been one of the most sustaining of my life. A onetime musician, he played the tenor sax at my wedding and has played no small part in my jazz education. We don't see everything the same way; Amadou is a shade or two more militant than I am (*Who isn't?* you're thinking). But he respects my views, and I respect his. So it was to Amadou that I sent my froth-covered email message. "You're right," he said, somewhat to my surprise, when we talked on the phone the next day. He added, though, that to sell this message to black people, there was one question I had to answer: With all that blacks have endured, and often still endure, at the hands of whites, what exactly will blacks get out of adopting my view? It's a good question that I've thought about a long time, and I'm sorry to say I don't have an answer that will persuade a lot of people. But I do have an answer.

One morning when I was in my early twenties, after graduating from college but before moving to New York, I stood talking to Ma near the open front door of 232, where I was living then. We saw a sixty-something woman walking up the street and recognized her as the sister of Mrs. Hansborough, our longtime neighbor at 230. She, the sister, looked as if her world had just collapsed. We stepped outside, and Ma called to the woman, who came up on our porch and said, "Sister died this morning." I understood that this was sad, and I stood there looking, I'm sure, appropriately solemn. But it was Ma who truly knew the score. She opened her arms, and Mrs. Hansborough's sister, whom we really didn't know very well, fell into them, crying like a small child. My mother said something to the effect that we would do anything we could for her, and the woman said through her tears, "You're here," comforting herself just a little.

Within months of that day, I was gone from 232, and you've already read what happened after that. In my late thirties, having fathered a pair of sisters, having seen them sleep side by side, laugh together, squabble occasionally, and snuggle with each other while watching TV, having seen these two little girls of mine form one of the strongest and most precious bonds of their lives, I finally understood what Ma had grasped instantly that day on the porch of 232.

I had become, like my mother before me, like every parent, a secret agent, discovering the same truths as every other agent, a discovery that must be made anew by each generation because it can never adequately be put into words. This knowledge operates as a lens, altering the appearance of the past and future. I looked back, for example, at that car crash on Division Avenue when I was little, at how Billy, Timmy, and I had run around playing in the aftermath of it, and how, today, I would have instead been wondering what my adult relatives out on the porch had no doubt wondered: what about the family in one of the cars? Were they okay? I looked back and asked myself why, when Wayne and our sixty-four-year-old mother visited me in Harlem in 1989, I responded with a laugh when Ma complained good-naturedly that I was walking her to death. Did I think she was still the woman in her late thirties who had brought me into the world? Did I think she would live forever?

She did not, and I will not. So here is my answer to Amadou's question: On the day that I go where my father, my mother, my grandmother, my aunts and uncles, Gerald Gladney, Selma Yampolsky, and Mrs. Hansborough have gone, if all goes as I pray it will, my children will be left behind. It is my hope that if they face times of crisis, the people around them, whatever their color, their sex, the sex of their lovers, will treat them with the understanding and compassion my mother showed Mrs. Hansborough's sister on that long-ago day. To have the right to that hope, I must try to treat others well, no matter what they look like. I finally learned as a young man that while thinking of others, it is important to look out for myself; as a man who has gotten older, I think of the lesson I absorbed from my family when I was a child: that while taking care of ourselves, we must also take care of others.

Often, in my dreams, I walk the streets of my childhood—hilly Division Avenue and its surrounding blocks and alleyways—as if no time has passed since I was that little boy asking where his mother went. The curious thing is that in my dreams I seldom, if ever, see people I know, as if, even in sleep, some part of me knows that they're gone.

Or maybe they're not there because in my waking life I have carried them all with me. Once in a while, a glass of straight bourbon in hand, I go to my living room and put on a record, *Coleman Hawkins and Roy Eldridge at the Opera House.* As I sit listening to those two men trade fours, as I hear the joy, camaraderie, and love in those exchanges of saxophone and trumpet, I think of my father and Uncle Brock; I remember my father's smooth voice and my uncle's rough, friendly one complementing each other, intersecting at points, as they marveled together over what was, what had been, what might be.

Acknowledgments

Many thanks are due to the following people, among others:

The hard-working staff and awards committee of the Mrs. Giles Whiting Foundation; my fellow editors Miriam Helbok and Mari Rich and my other comrades-in-arms at The H. W. Wilson Company, who made my day-to-day life pleasant while I wrote most of this book; Sally, Brooks, and Judy Peck, Mark Sanders, Kevin and the Conroy/Nordals, David ("Jazz Santa") Ochshorn and family, the Pang/Ressners, Claire Weissberg, Mishi Faruqee, Laura Miller, Stew, Andre Robert Lee, and the other great people who are not mentioned in this book but whose friendship has helped keep me going over the years; Michael Simms, Caroline Tanski, Christine Stroud, Chris Duerr, and Giuliana Certo of Autumn House Press, for giving my work a home and offering warm guidance through the publication process; and those who read and advised me on drafts of this book, providing much encouragement: Phillip Lopate, Thomas Rayfiel, Charles Hawley, and my wife, Amy Peck.

Brief portions of this book originally appeared elsewhere. Passages from Chapter 1 were published in the essays "On Unhappiness, Friendship, and Charlie Brown" in *The Reading Room*, Issue Six, 2006, and "For Dean" in *The Threepenny Review*, Spring 2003. Parts of Chapter 3 originally appeared as "Sugar, Muhammad, and Me" in *The Threepenny Review*, Spring 1999, and Chapter 4 (Interlude) was published in longer form as a Table Talk piece in *The Threepenny Review*, Spring 2009. Brief sections of Chapter 5 were published first in the Summer 2001 *Threepenny Review* essay "Memories of an Ex-Would-Be Cartoonist." Sections of Chapter 11 first appeared in the essays "Race and Anger" in *Commonweal*, February

23, 1996, and "How I Became Black," in *The Reading Room*, Issue Four, 2002. Part of Chapter 17 was published, in different form, in the essay "Black and American: What Does It Mean?" in *Commonweal*, February 13, 1998. Finally, a passage in Chapter 19 originally appeared in "For Dean."

The Autumn House Nonfiction Series

Michael Simms, General Editor

Twin of Blackness: A Memoir
Clifford Thompson

So Many Africas: Six Years in a Zambian Village
Jill Kandel • 2014

A Greater Monster
Adam Patric Miller • 2013

Bear Season: A Journey into Ursidae
Katherine Ayres

Love for Sale and Other Essays
Clifford Thompson • 2012

Between Song and Story: Essays for the Twenty-first Century
Sheryl St. Germain and Margaret L. Whitford, eds.

Archipelago: A Balkan Passage
Robert Isenberg

• Winner of the Autumn House Nonfiction Prize

Design and Production

Text and cover design by Kathy Boykowycz

Cover painting by Clifford Thompson; photographed by Amadou Diallo

Author photo by Kate Slininger

Set in Frutiger fonts, designed in 1975 by Adrian Frutiger

Printed by McNaughton and Gunn, Saline, Michigan